Critical Perspectives on Language and Kinship in Multilingual Families

Also available from Bloomsbury

Becoming a Citizen, by Kamran Khan
Communicating with the Public, edited by Hansun Zhang Waring and Elizabeth Reddington
Identity in Applied Linguistics Research, by Lisa McEntee-Atalianis
Language, Identity and Symbolic Culture, by David Evans
The Cultural Memory of Language, by Susan Samata
The Sociopolitics of English Language Testing, edited by Seyyed-Abdolhamid Mirhosseini and Peter De Costa

Critical Perspectives on Language and Kinship in Multilingual Families

Lyn Wright

BLOOMSBURY ACADEMIC
LONDON · NEW YORK · OXFORD · NEW DELHI · SYDNEY

BLOOMSBURY ACADEMIC
Bloomsbury Publishing Plc
50 Bedford Square, London, WC1B 3DP, UK
1385 Broadway, New York, NY 10018, USA
29 Earlsfort Terrace, Dublin 2, Ireland

BLOOMSBURY, BLOOMSBURY ACADEMIC and the Diana logo
are trademarks of Bloomsbury Publishing Plc

First published in Great Britain 2020
This paperback edition published 2022

Copyright © Lyn Wright, 2020

Lyn Wright has asserted her right under the Copyright, Designs
and Patents Act, 1988, to be identified as Author of this work.

For legal purposes the Acknowledgments on p. ix constitute
an extension of this copyright page.

All rights reserved. No part of this publication may be reproduced or transmitted
in any form or by any means, electronic or mechanical, including photocopying,
recording, or any information storage or retrieval system, without
prior permission in writing from the publishers.

Bloomsbury Publishing Plc does not have any control over, or responsibility for,
any third-party websites referred to or in this book. All internet addresses given
in this book were correct at the time of going to press. The author and publisher
regret any inconvenience caused if addresses have changed or sites have
ceased to exist, but can accept no responsibility for any such changes.

A catalogue record for this book is available from the British Library.

Library of Congress Cataloging-in-Publication Data
Names: Wright, Lyn (Eveyln), author.
Title: Critical perspectives on language and kinship in multilingual
families / Lyn Wright.
Description: London, UK ; New York, NY : Bloomsbury Academic, 2020. |
Includes bibliographical references and index.
Identifiers: LCCN 2020020642 (print) | LCCN 2020020643 (ebook) |
ISBN 9781350088283 (hardback) | ISBN 9781350088290 (ebook) |
ISBN 9781350088306 (epub)
Subjects: LCSH: Language in families. | Multilingualism–Social aspects.
Classification: LCC P40.5.F36 W75 2020 (print) | LCC P40.5.F36
(ebook) | DDC 306.44085–dc23
LC record available at https://lccn.loc.gov/2020020642
LC ebook record available at https://lccn.loc.gov/2020020643

ISBN:	HB:	978-1-3500-8828-3
	PB:	978-1-3502-0364-8
	ePDF:	978-1-3500-8829-0
	eBook:	978-1-3500-8830-6

Typeset by Integra Software Services Pvt. Ltd.

To find out more about our authors and books visit www.bloomsbury.com
and sign up for our newsletters.

This book is dedicated to Noah, Amy, and Fanghorne
"They don't have to be issued from my tissue to be mine"
—*Sister Peace*

Contents

List of Figures and Tables		viii
Acknowledgments		ix
Note on Transcription		xi
1	Toward a Critical Approach to Family Language	1
2	Why Are Single Parents Good at Using a Minority Language?: Talking about and to Kids	29
3	Walking to School in Russian: Constructing a Mother-Daughter Relationship	55
4	Adoptive Families: Constructing Competence, History, and Knowledge	79
5	Gender, Sexuality, and Bilingualism in the LGBTQ+-Identified Family	101
6	The Monolingual, Nuclear Family: Erasing Melania Trump	119
7	Researching and Supporting All Families	139
References		154
Index		166

List of Figures and Tables

Figure

2.1	Percentage of Questions	40

Tables

2.1	Interview Participants	46
2.2	'We' and 'Us' in Interviews	48
2.3	'We' and 'Us' in Interviews with Kevin Excluded	49
2.4	Interpretable Referents of "we/us" as Percent of Total Mentions by Parents	49
3.1	Walk-to-School Recordings	62
3.2	Topics of Conversation on the Walk to School	63
6.1	Sources and Headlines	123
6.2	List of All Kinship Terms/Family References Coded	125

Acknowledgments

In the summer of 2017, I traveled to London on vacation and ended up giving a talk at Birkbeck College on family language policy. I am very grateful to my good friend Jia Jackie Lou who suggested the event and Zhu Hua who made the official invitation and organized an amazing session. I would like to thank Gurdeep Mattu for the forward thinking that led to turning that talk into a book-length volume and Andrew Wardell who has provided much guidance through the editorial process. Becky Holland has kept me on track and answered numerous questions. Without Bloomsbury and Birkbeck College, this book would not have happened.

Kendall King remains an inspirational mentor and role model. I am honored to have been able to work with her closely over the last ten years. I appreciate her valuable input in this project.

I received support from the University of Memphis through two grants to conduct the research and write the manuscript. In 2017–18 I received a Faculty Research Grant from the College of Arts and Sciences for a study of Russian-speaking mothers. In the spring of 2019, I was awarded a Marcus Orr Center for the Humanities (MOCH) Fellowship. My MOCH colleagues (Remy Debes, Nikki Detraz, Sarah Potter, and Cookie Woolner) provided tremendous support and read an early version of the Melania Trump chapter. I also need to thank my English department colleagues who all work to create a stimulating academic environment in which this work was produced. Graduate students Muna Alosaimi, Fahad Alzahrani, and Emil Ubaldo helped me with transcribing the data for some sections of these projects and proofreading the manuscript.

I am privileged to belong to an active, international research community that has engaged with many of the ideas and discussion in this book. I thank Åsa Palviainen for continued discussion and research with diverse families and involvement in the WhatsInApp? project in Finland. Symposia and colloquia organized by and with Xiao Lan Curdt-Christiansen, Christina Higgins, Elizabeth Lanza, and Li Wei have all been instrumental in helping me think about and research these issues.

Many sections of this book emerged from conversations I had with friends and acquaintances. I am grateful to Katerina Sedra for intense discussion about post-Soviet kinships, Bonnie Locklear for her perspectives on Lumbee kinship, and Ruth Goldman for introducing me to the documentary about Del LaGrace Volcano.

My own academic-social network of fellow parents has supported me: Esra Ozdenerol, Cameron Fogle, and all the single and married parents who carpool, meet at basketball games, and arrange play dates. I also thank the Magnolia Sangha and Magnolia Grove Meditation Center for providing healing spaces for the practice of mindfulness.

Finally, I need and want to thank the numerous parents and children who have talked with me, recorded their conversations for me, and reviewed transcripts and data with me (and corrected my Russian!). It is time to hear all of their voices.

Note on Transcription

Transcription conventions

(Adapted from Tannen, Kendall, and Gordon [2007])

Line breaks indicate the end of an utterance

(.)	noticeable pause
[	brackets indicate overlapping speech
CAPS	emphatic stress
::	vowel or consonant lengthening
-	speaker retraces or self-corrects
hhh	laughter
/???/	unintelligible word or phrase
<crying>	nonverbal vocalization
( )	comment by analyst
.	at the end of utterance falling intonation
,	at the end of utterance continuing or slight rising intonation
?	at end of utterance rising intonation, not necessarily a question
!	at end of utterance animated intonation, not necessarily exclamation

1

Toward a Critical Approach to Family Language

Why are single mothers particularly good at raising bilingual children? How do transnational adoptive families create new kinships and shared histories across time, space, and language? When does bilingualism unite and divide LGBTQ+-identified families, and how do translingual resources facilitate new gender roles and relationships in the family? And finally, when and why is family multilingualism erased in the public sphere in the US and other national contexts? This book examines the kinship and language processes in diverse, non-normative families (i.e., single parent, adoptive, and LGBTQ+) as well as the construction of public discursive norms about family through analysis of interactional, interview, and news media data. The twenty-first century has ushered in a renewed interest in kinship in social sciences (de Pina-Cabral and Leutloff-Grandits, 2012; Furstenburg, 2020; Homans, 2018), and this book demonstrates how examining kinship processes (e.g., routine caregiving activities, talk about family, and the use, negotiation, and formation of kinship terms) in the bi- and multilingual family can bring to the foreground not only the role of language negotiations in exclusion, inclusion, and belonging in the family but also the importance of gender roles and sexual identities in family language processes. Kinship approaches to family bi- and multilingualism embed language development and use in larger family projects where bi- and multilingualism both construct and are constructed by kinships and, in some cases, are erased in favor of a monolingual, nuclear family norm.

The families I present in the research studies that follow in this book are similar to many of the family members I have met in my work and daily life over the past ten years. Sometimes, the people in my everyday life offer more diverse and complex stories than my research participants. A student in the first university class that I taught in Mississippi tells me how she learned Russian in the early 2000s from her three adopted siblings in order to bond with them and negotiate her place in the growing family. Matteo, a contractor and builder, tells me how he gives his teenage children life advice on FaceTime calls to Mexico. My queer friends in Estonia provide a hub for a large community of bisexual and lesbian Russian-speaking women who raise their children using three languages: Russian, Estonian, and English. My friend Inna arrived in the United States through marriage migration with her teenage son from Crimea. Her son returned to Crimea, but she is now remarried and parenting a Russian-English bilingual child. Elena, a single mother who participated in one of the studies of this book, tells me she and her parents are proud of her daughter's Russian competence and the importance of Russian in their relationship. These families represent contemporary, twenty-first-century bi- and multilingual family configurations (single parent, adoptive, queer, transgender) who have rarely found a central voice in research on multilingual families, bilingual parenting, and family language policy despite the potential theoretical, not to mention ethical and methodological, contributions such families can make. This book focuses on kinship processes and the formation of family roles and relationships in multilingual single parent, adoptive, and queer families in order to demonstrate how multilingualism is related to discursive acts of doing family.

A survey of contemporary media can also show how diverse the multilingual family landscape has become in public life in the United States (and potentially around the world). In a 2018 article for *Paste* magazine, Gunderson notes that bilingual families are on the rise in broadcast television in the United States thanks to shows like *Jane the Virgin*, *Fresh off the Boat*, and *Speechless* that air on services such as Netflix and are "changing the cultural conversation" about non-English and bilingual programming. Shows such as *Jane the Virgin* are important because of not only the bilingualism present on the screen, but also the diversity and complexity of family relations portrayed. Like the friends and acquaintances I have met and talked to about bilingual parenting, school choices, and language, the focal family of the show is diverse, made up of three generations of bilingual Spanish-English-speaking women who are all single mothers as well as a second, related new immigrant mother from the Czech Republic. The show touches on topics of in-vitro fertilization, co-parenting, bisexuality and coming out, and transnationalism that are hallmarks of twenty-first-century families and parenting processes, as do many contemporary popular television shows and movies around the world.

For all the friends, acquaintances, students, research participants, public figures, and even fictional characters who talk about their experiences in multilingual families, it is usually the family, and not language, that comes first. Matteo wanted to give advice to his grown son about money, my Russian Estonian friends wanted their children to feel accepted and loved, the biological sister to three Russian adoptees wanted to negotiate her place in her own family. This seeming generalization, that most families are interested in being and doing family more than they are interested in language and that family roles and relationships take priority over language choice, seems to be key to understanding multilingualism in the family.

However, prioritizing *family* or kinship in multilingual family studies is completely at odds with the ways in which family bi- and multilingualism have traditionally been studied by linguists. Most studies of bilingual parenting, family language policy, and multilingual families (including some of my own) take language as the analytical focus. Such studies have carefully examined how family members use language, the bi- and multilingual competencies of family members, and the language ideologies that shape such use. Why then are linguists so reluctant to embrace the diverse, complex, and sometimes-contradictory multilingual families that make up contemporary society? My answer to this question, in a nutshell, is that most socio- and applied linguists, while acknowledging that diversity exists in multilingual families, do not have the theoretical and methodological tools to address the complex, intersectional processes that occur in single parent, adoptive, and queer multilingual families and have side-stepped the issue with the assumption that these families do not represent the norm or the majority of multilingual families (cf. similar discussions in Coetzee, 2018; Fogle, 2012; Navarro and Macalister, 2016; Obied, 2010). In this volume, I demonstrate how a discursive focus on kinship and analysis of how family members talk about family and use kinship terms, how they engage in family routines, and how they negotiate roles and relationships can facilitate an understanding of bi- and multilingual language use. In this volume, I examine where the family formation processes occur first and then look for the use of minority or heritage language or bi- and multilingualism.

In her groundbreaking book on queer and Latinx identities, Cashman (2017: 25) calls for a queering of bilingualism studies in an effort to make the minority central and minimize the focus on the "hypothetical future child" to better understand the bilingual lives of all individuals. While the current volume is focused on families with parents and children, I center the minorities within the minority (i.e., single parent, adoptive, and queer multilingual families) to bring to the forefront issues of kinship, gender and sexuality, and relationship building in the study of multilingual language use and learning in the family. In my view, these constructs (kinship, gender, sexuality, and relationships) are central to understanding bi- and multilingual language use, family language policy, and language shift.

This volume brings together work in family discourse, family language socialization, and family language policy to demonstrate how kinship in so-called non-normative families is constructed through talk about family, everyday routines, and multilingual language use. Drawing on contemporary practice-based and critical approaches to kinship studies, I argue that the family is discursively constructed in interaction (Tannen et al., 2007) and that multilingual resources along with other interactional strategies play a role in these processes. The findings from interview, interactional, and public discourse studies contribute to an overall examination of processes of inclusion and exclusion, caregiving, and relationship and role formation that make up kinships as discussed further below and depend on bi- and multilingual language resources. The analyses here offer new avenues and techniques for considering multilingualism in the family as well as the complex, and often non-linear, processes of language maintenance and shift that is at the heart of work on bi- and multilingual families.

Aim of the Volume

The study of multilingual family language and interaction has burgeoned in the past decades with researchers interested in family identities, relationships, multilingualism, and socialization building new insights into parent-child interaction and the language practices and ideologies at home that intersect with societal multilingualism and language maintenance and shift (for recent reviews of multilingual family and family language policy research, see King, 2016; King and Lanza, 2017; Smith-Christmas, 2016). This book contributes to current work on multilingual (and monolingual) family language by taking a more careful look at "family" or kinship in linguistic processes. How does language use contribute to constructing family identities and relationships? How are kinships constructed in interaction and discourse? By focusing on non-normative families such as adoptive, single parent, and LGBTQ+-identified families who engage in quotidian negotiations of what it means to be family and are conscious of the project of being and becoming family, the studies in this book show how including the perspective of more diverse family types and kinship processes in the study of multilingual family language contributes to understanding family discourse and socialization processes.

This book addresses two primary issues in the study of multilingual families and family language policy identified by King and Fogle (2017). First, the primary goal of this volume is to expand the "who" of family language studies by focusing on single parent, adoptive, and queer-identified families. The studies in this volume demonstrate how theoretical consideration of the interactional and discursive consequences of family configuration can expand discussions of bilingual parenting, child agency, and gender and sexuality in the family. Further, focusing on kinship processes in non-normative multilingual families leads to understanding multilingual resources in relation to family relationships and roles, taking the field beyond ethnolinguistic identities and language ideologies to a better understanding of relationships, gender, and sexuality in relation to family language.

Second, the volume draws on diverse data sets and methodologies to examine the construction of family and kinship relations through language. By working with interview, interactional, and public discourse data from a variety of different sites (from participants' homes to popular film), the studies in this book address different scales and domains of the production of family and intersections of language ideologies, practices, and management (Spolsky, 2004). Integrating language socialization, family discourse, family language policy, and nexus analysis research further allows for multidimensional perspectives on multilingual families and kinship processes.

In order to develop a more critical stance toward the notion of "family" and the process of doing and creating family in family language research, I incorporate perspectives from critical kinship studies that focus on kinship as action and discourse. In the analyses, language is considered a resource for constructing family and kinship, and the family is viewed as dynamic and negotiated. Kinship entails and includes caregiving practices and affective relations, but perhaps more relevant to the study of bi- and multilingualism and bi- and multilingual families, as Franklin and McKinnon (2002) note, kinship is a process of inclusion and exclusion. Kinships occur both within and outside of families, and certain kinships are valued while others are hidden. That is, biology neither determines nor predicts kinship—children lose touch of birth mothers and adults make kin with strangers. Kinship processes depend on linguistic and discursive processes, and the role of language comes to light in families where kinship is discussed, negotiated, and done in ways that fall outside of a perceived norm.

In this introduction, I will start with an overview of research on multilingual families and family language policy and argue for the inclusion of diverse family structures to expand this field of study. I will then provide context for the studies in this volume with a discussion of contemporary approaches to the study of kinship and how practice-based and critical kinship approaches can facilitate the study of family language. I then turn to three types of family language studies (family discourse, family language socialization, and family language policy) to discuss how different theories and methodologies can come together to present a more complex view of language in multilingual families. I will then introduce the studies that are presented in the chapters.

The Study of Bi- and Multilingual Families

There are two main questions that have guided the study of bilingual (and to a lesser extent multilingual) families over the past fifty years or so. First, why do some children growing up in a bilingual family achieve high levels of competence in both languages while others do not (De Houwer, 1999; Lanza, 1997/2004)? And second, how do linguistic practices in the family explain societal-level language maintenance and shift (Canagarajah, 2008; Smith-Christmas, 2014; Spolsky, 2012)? The first question emerged from a psycholinguistic approach to childhood bilingualism and bilingual first acquisition, and the second is tied more closely to the fields of language policy and reversing language shift (Fishman, 1991) intended to understand how communities lose languages and how they can reverse that process. In a series of articles, Kendall King and colleagues argued that bringing these two areas of study together under the rubric of family language policy could integrate psycholinguistic and language policy perspectives to better understand three main areas of family multilingualism, following Spolsky (2004), that is, language ideologies, practices, and management, and would shed light on the complex processes involved in children's bilingual development and language shift (King et al., 2008).

The family language policy approach has provided valuable insights into the interactional patterns associated with language maintenance and shift (Gafaranga, 2010; Smith-Christmas, 2014), the role of child agency in home interactions (Fogle, 2012; Gyogi, 2014; Said and Zhu Hua, 2017), similarities (and differences) of family language policies processes in varied contexts, and the fact that family language policies are dynamic and can be both implicit and explicit (Curdt-Christiansen, 2009; van Mensel, 2018). However, as King and Fogle (2017) noted, family language policy research, designed to understand language processes in bi- and multilingual families, has had significant blind spots. King and Fogle argued that family language policy might be better served to abandon the narrow focus on ideologies, practices, and management (that seems to replicate similar analyses across contexts, namely, similar strategies and ideologies that lead to passive or productive competence) and take more of a language socialization approach. Language socialization research is founded on the notion that children learn language through culture and culture through language (Ochs and Schieffelin, 1984). Language socialization affords the field of family language policy a more contextualized, in-depth understanding of multilingualism in the family by expanding examinations of identities, roles, and sociocultural norms in relation to family language use and children's language development.

Other scholars working in the fields of family language policy and multilingual family communication more generally have noted a need for shifts in perspective and approach. More recent studies have noted that multilingualism is experienced differently for individual families and family members as Zhu Hua and Li Wei (2016: 665) noted in their study of Chinese-speaking families in the UK:

> Recognising the diversity of transnational families and the experiences of different generations and individuals within the families has significant implications for policy, practice and research … In research, bilingualism and multilingualism need to be studied as *experience,* and experiences need to be studied holistically and multidimensionally.

King and Lanza (2017: 2) also note a shifting focus to family construction:

> Researchers are increasingly interested in how families are constructed through multilingual language practices, and how language functions as a resource for this process of family making and meaning-making in contexts of transmigration, social media and technology saturation, and hypermobility.

Further, the predominate focus on small children does not adequately capture the diverse and complex multilingual processes that involve not only intergenerational transmission of languages but also individuals' identities and experiences outside of family life (Cashman, 2017). The calls to focus on individual experiences in the family, language as a resource for family making, and experiences outside of the family can be examined through the lens of kinship.

One important debate in family multilingualism studies (and family language policy) centers on the extent to which studies of bi- and multilingualism should focus on linguistic outcomes for children and the association of those outcomes with family interaction vs. the multilingual experiences that family members have. These two approaches take different views on the family as a context for development vs. a construct that is dynamic and changing with the changing child.

King (2016) noted that both the outcomes and experiences perspectives hold merit and allow for greater insight into the role of multilingual family language. While the fields of family language policy and multilingual parenting are turning to more complex considerations of meaning-making in multilingual families, King argued that integration of outcomes-based and meaning- or experience-based approaches will best serve educational and policy-making needs. In this book, I explore how widening the focus of multilingual family studies to a study of kinship processes can engage both context (outcomes) and construct (experiences) approaches. Kinship processes contextualize language phenomena and mediate both the relationship between family member interaction and cultural norms and practices, as well as the perceived dichotomy of outcomes vs. experiences.

This exploration into the construction of multilingual kinships opens new avenues to understanding how family configuration influences interactional patterns, how children's agencies and competencies are constructed, the role of gender and sexuality in family multilingual processes, and the role of relationships and caregiving in multilingual use and development. In the following sections, I outline first the family language studies that have focused on non-normative families as a way to elucidate kinship processes in the context of the multilingual family, and then I turn to approaches to kinship and family that inform the analyses of multilingual language use and argue for a critical family language studies that is inclusive, multidimensional, and contextualized.

Diverse Multilingual Families

Diversity can refer to a variety of identity- (and competence-) related factors, including but not limited to ethnicity, race, gender, sexual orientation, and disability status. When I refer to diverse families in this book, I am typically talking about families that fall outside of a nuclear, two-parents-with-children norm (although this perceived norm may actually be a myth as historian Stephanie Coontz [2016] notes). While racial, ethnic, and ethnolinguistic diversities are very important aspects of the study of multilingual families, and studies conducted with transnational and extended families have demonstrated language processes in some types of non-nuclear families especially extended, multi-generational families (Curdt-Christiansen, 2013; King, 2013; Smith-Christmas, 2016), this book focuses on non-normative family configurations that have more to do with diverse kinships, gender roles, and sexualities. Family construction is ongoing in all families (as family discourse studies have noted [Tannen et al., 2007]), but it is more evident in families that consciously negotiate societal norms and pre-existing expectations about family in their everyday interactions.

Multilingual family studies have begun to examine more diverse types of families in contexts outside of the Western, nuclear family that have typically been studied in this field as mentioned above. Recent studies of multilingual families, for example, have included multigenerational families with grandparents and extended family members (Higgins, 2019; Smith-Christmas, 2014; Zhu Hua and Li Wei, 2016), single parented families (Navarro and McAlister, 2016), sibling-headed (Kendrick and Namazzi, 2016), and adoptive families (Fogle, 2012; Shin, 2013). These studies have focused on the affective experiences of family members in multilingual interactions, suggesting that the emotional bonds formed in the family are important to language use and maintenance. As Kendrick and Namazzi (2016: 71) noted in their study of child-headed families in Uganda:

> We would argue that, in many ways, the implicit language policies evident in the four child-headed families are often emotionally driven and serve as a coping mechanism. Their policies and ways of using language help the children to protect the family unit against further loss and to minimise emotional distress.

For these families who formed out of traumatic circumstances, language practices were tied to the emotional aspects of negotiating stress and distress. These emotional processes are further part of doing kinship as language is tied to caregiving and belonging as discussed below.

Despite the fact that more diverse families and contexts are represented in the family language policy and multilingual family literature, there is little discussion of how family structure or the need to form and maintain kinships over space and time relates to multilingual language use in the family (cf. Palviainen, 2020). Including and focusing on diverse families is a way to center structural, affective, and interactional differences in multilingual family processes. In particular, perspectives from the field of critical kinship studies (Franklin and McKinnon, 2002; Krølokke et al., 2016) can expand the study of multilingual families by focusing on the primary processes in the family of constructing relationships, inclusion and exclusion, and caregiving and embedding linguistic analyses within this perspective.

Kinship Studies

The study of kinship has seen a renewed and growing interest in the early twenty-first century in response to the perceived changing demographics of families and new family formation processes. As Furstenberg (2020: 364) notes, contemporary trends include growing family complexity, cohabitation as an alternative to marriage, assisted reproduction, and voluntary childlessness, all of which suggest a need for greater attention to kinship processes outside of the nuclear family. Other scholars point to adoption and same-sex families as both reproducing and transforming traditional family norms through new kinship processes (Homans, 2018). And this is not just in Western, industrialized contexts. Singerman (2007), for example, noted that women in the Middle East were waiting longer to have children, a trend that is also seen in the United States.

Much of the early work in kinship studies was rooted in the anthropologically based study of language and terminology. As Fox (1984) noted in her contemporary overview of the field, up until that time 50 percent of kinship studies (including influential works of Henry Lewis Morgan (1871/1997) and Lévi-Strauss (1969)) had been studies of kinship terminology and thus had a language-based (but perhaps not linguistic) approach. Morgan, for example, had spent decades charting the kinship terminology of the Iroquois and other Native American tribes to work out a system for understanding social institutions. Lévi-Strauss (1949) further examined kinship in Indigenous groups through marriage practices and terminologies. The central notion in this language-based approach was that to understand the classification of kinship relations (as substantiated in language and kinship terms) in a given society was to understand the actual relationships and structures of the society itself. This structural approach (i.e., that an existing term signified an existing relationship), however, was critiqued in its susceptibility to interpretation and ethnocentrism as tribal cultures were often compared to Anglo Saxon norms (Franklin and McKinnon, 2002). Further, other scholars, such as Malinowski (1930), argued for a practice-based approach to kinship as Fox (1984: 240) noted that, "Malinowski despised 'kinship algebra', as he called the study of terms, and many anthropologists follow him in this distaste insisting that what we should study is 'behavior' or 'rules' and not language." It is this practice-based approach that can inform studies of multilingual families and, concomitantly, to which linguists can contribute through discourse analytic approaches.

In this volume, I take a social constructionist approach to kinship that views kinship as something that is done rather than something that is determined by biology (genetic or blood relations) or marriage. Biology cannot explain the kinship relations formed between adoptive parents and children, and marriage does not adequately account for the human relations that count as kin. Critical kinship studies typically focus on relationships that are formed in the context of adoption, IVF treatment, and same-sex parented families among the other myriad context in which people feel as kin (e.g., the Buddhist sangha, queer social networks, families with paid caregivers, or close-knit friend groups). Biological and marital definitions of kinship, further, do not explain how some parents reject or disown their children as in the case of queer and trans youths who form chosen families (Cashman, 2017). As I have argued elsewhere (Fogle, 2012), studying the linguistic processes involved in forming family or kinship in families where kinship is not taken as a biological fact can help to understand how these processes occur in all families and the relationship of language, language development, and multilingualism to kinship and family.

Kinship as Practice

Current kinship studies take a practice-based approach and see kinship as "negotiated." Practice-based studies focus on the ways in which kinship is invoked as a way to protect and enact power and to create both inclusion and exclusion (Franklin and McKinnon, 2002). Such approaches call for the detachment of kinship from biological processes and focus on human behavior and action as Franklin and McKinnon note here:

> It is not simply that kinship must always be created, negotiated, and brought into being in practice …. It is also that the lines between kinship and other forms of relationally are fluid … On the one hand, friends, villagers, religious associates, "radicalized" others, and strangers can be made into kin, while mothers, grandparents, and patrilineal relations can be made into strangers, or "just" friends. (p. 13)

In fact, Gauthier and Moody (2014), in their study of the formation of kinship, have presented arguments for seeing family as "activity" and "experience." In this approach, kinship is constructed through the linguistic practices and other actions in the family or in the making of family, and individual family members have their own subjective experience with these practices and socialization processes. Adoptive families are formed through legal documents and language, gender roles and parent status are negotiated through storytelling and other interactive events at home (Ochs and Taylor, 1995), and family members are included or excluded by language choice and multilingual language use (Zhu Hua, 2015). These are all examples of how a discursive approach to kinship can illuminate language in the family.

In further discussion, Franklin and McKinnon (2002: 15) note that inclusion and exclusion are integral processes in the formation of kinships:

> Kinship systems, like gender, have often been theorized as classification systems and even as grammars. In turn, such social technologies of naming and classifying, or of sorting and dividing, are seen to be generative of the kinds of material, relational, and cultural worlds that are possible, and for whom. As a classificatory technology, kinship can be mobilized to signify not only specific kinds of connection and inclusion but also specific kinds of disconnection and exclusion.

Viewing kinship as a process of inclusion and exclusion connects with the study of multilingualism in the family where languages and language competencies can divide or bring together family members. This approach further entails an analysis of the functions of kinship terminology and explicit talk about kinship in family discourse. Reference to a kinship role or relation (e.g., calling "Mom!" in interaction as the daughter in Chapter 3 does on the walk to school or referring to Donald Trump as "Melania Trump's husband" in a news article in Chapter 6) can accomplish a number of interactional functions and construct kinship relations that are relevant to the understanding of inclusion and exclusion in the family as can using one language or the other to include or exclude certain family members as I discuss in Chapter 5.

Further, taking a discursive approach to kinship allows for kinships to be constructed outside of biological processes. Tovares (2010), for example, has shown that even the family dog becomes kin through linguistic practices. Viewing kinship processes as a contextualized set of actions, behaviors, or practices that are closely related to establishing in-group and out-group identities or memberships coincides with contemporary linguistic discussions over belonging, language learning, and language socialization in which language development and learning are intertwined with learning sociocultural norms and identities. Taken a step further, kinship is an intermediary step in the reproduction or transformation of cultural norms as discussed in the study of language socialization (e.g., Kulick, 1997). Non-normative families are negotiated families (Fogle, 2012; Poveda et al., 2014) and as the parent-child kinship roles are transformed so too are the sociocultural and sociolinguistic norms from one generation to the next.

Critical Kinship Studies

Critical kinship studies, according to recent volumes by Kroløkke et al. (2016) and Riggs and Peele (2016), refer to the study of the social construction of kinship relations in contexts or families where a biological or "natural" parent-child relationship is not available or assumed, that is, in cases of adoption, same-sex parenting, or parenting through the use of technology and in some cases single parenting. From a linguistic perspective, such families are discursively constructed through explicit talk about family belonging and everyday routines and practices. Poveda et al. (2014), for example, demonstrated how single-mothers-by-choice focused on talking about being a family in their everyday conversations with their children. Fogle (2012) offered analysis of how three adoptive families did family by engaging in routine linguistic practices such as storytelling or metalinguistic talk. Thus from a kinship perspective, language socialization and family language policy studies could reimagine the interactional practices associated with language development and multilingual competence (e.g., narrative, metalinguistic talk, and translanguaging) as more complexly related to forging and negotiating kinships. Critical kinship studies focus on the family-as-action, or family-as-construct, in a variety of different settings. In migratory contexts, kinship is often reconfigured. In a study of Masaai adoptees in Kenya, for example, Archambault (2010: 229) demonstrated how children "play an active role in the making and unmaking of kinship" and how they resist normative representations of family as a fixed entity.

A related area of kinship studies examines how kinship can be defined as caregiving. In the context of immigration, Flores (2018: 475) carefully documented the intersections of caregiving and education specifically in constructing kinship relations. In her study, she demonstrated how older sisters in Latino, immigrant-origin families provide caregiving to younger siblings and "complicate genealogical generation by pointing to how generations are created not just by descent but also by care practices, like education," or what she called "the descendant bargain." Flores pointed out that education is central to the immigrant experience, and providing educational support intimately tied with kinship roles and parenting. While the studies in the current volume do not focus on sibling relationships, Chapters 2 and 3 do point to literacy practices (e.g., educational caregiving) and the connection to parent-child relationships. This relationship between sibling care and education can also be found in applied linguistic work such as Hawkins's (2005) study of two elementary school-aged boys, one whose sister helped him after school and facilitated his affiliation with school culture. King (2016) has further examined sibling relationships in transnational families. Learning and teaching a language at home can be a form of kinship formation as it is seen as a caregiving practice.

Bi- and multilingual competences further intersect with sexual identities and kinship relations (Cashman, 2017; Wright, 2017). Lesbian, gay, queer, and trans-identified individuals report forming "chosen families" in place of biological families of origin often out of necessity. In Cashman's (2017) volume on queer, bilingual Latinx identities, one participant in particular (Mario) discussed leaving his biological family for a chosen queer family because of the need for freedom and identity despite his undocumented status. These choices and formation of new kinships were related to the construction of an English-speaking, rather than Spanish-speaking world for Mario; however, he reported that his English as a Second Language status at school as a child also influenced his own personal shift to English. Other studies focusing on queer identities and migration have further shown how kinship ties are reformulated in this context, and such reimaginings of kinships have significance for racial, cultural, and linguistic identities (Eng, 2010).

A large body of work has further investigated online kinships, which is not a focal area of the current volume, but relevant to these studies. Andreassan (2016) examined how online communities allowed for the formation of "new kinship relations" in donor families where a sperm or egg was donated by an individual. Enriquez (2016) found that so-called quick media cannot replace face-to-face interaction for kinship building for undocumented second-generation Mexican immigrants who tried to maintain kinship ties through social media across national boundaries. These participants reported feeling distanced from relatives in Mexico and did not establish the belonging they were seeking. These findings point to a need for close study of face-to-face interaction in families (something that sociolinguists and linguistic anthropologists have been particularly successful at doing) in comparison to media use to better understand how kinship is formed and what makes the day-to-day routine similar to and different from other ways of interacting. In sum, studies that focus on kinship, literacy, and language centralize kinship as a process of doing or an action (i.e., educational caregiving, choosing family, interacting) where the role of bi- and multilingual socialization is contextualized in a complex process of relationship and identity building that individuals negotiate in migratory and multilingual contexts.

Who's Your People?

A final example of how practice-based and critical kinship approaches can facilitate an understanding of language in the family comes from Indigenous contexts in North America. According to anthropologist David Wilkins (2018), kinship can be a particularly fraught construct in relation to Indigenous communities in post-colonial settings as claiming tribal membership and access to resources associated with membership is legally tied to blood lines and genetic authenticity by federal laws. In a discussion of the tribal enrollment process of the Lumbee Tribe of North Carolina, Wilkins notes that members of the Lumbee community themselves do not rely on DNA tests, residence status, or knowledge of Lumbee places (all part of the official membership process) to determine membership and kinship. Rather, Wilkins notes Lumbee ask one another a question "Who's your people?" as a way of greeting that "link[s] us [Lumbee] together as a community." This question begins the process of identifying each other as members of the tribe and citizens through talk about family members and relationships, and creates a discursive network that represents belonging and the ties of inclusion. In the face of erasure and exclusion, "Who's your people" is an important resource for connecting family and community, tribal belonging and inclusion. The

Lumbee example demonstrates how talking about kinship relations and roles is one way that people do family, belonging, and citizenship. This social and discursive construction of kin is at the center of the current book.

Approaches to Kinship in This Volume

In sum, contemporary studies of kinship examine these processes in relation to practices, activities, and experiences associated with caregiving and inclusion or belonging. Kinship in this book is studied from a linguistic, discourse analytic and interactional sociolinguistic perspective. By identifying language practices in which family members engage that are associated with relationship building, caregiving, and identity, I demonstrate how belonging (and sometimes exclusion) is constructed in families, how non-nuclear and non-normative families are created through language, and what multilingual resources or interactions are associated with these processes.

In specific, this volume examines the linguistic construction of kinships through the use of kinship terms, engagement in interactional routines and patterns, and explicit talk about family and being family. In Chapters 3 and 6, I consider the function of kinship terms in discourse, both in the public sphere and in the private family interactions. The interactional and discursive functions of kinship terms are rarely discussed in sociolinguistic research, but deserve greater attention in understanding how normative families are constructed in public discourse as well as how they are used interactionally in family conversations. Following work in language socialization, a second area of kinship formation that I consider is the use of interactional routines or patterns of language use in the family. This plane of analysis weaves throughout the chapters, as kinship terms, for example, can be a part of a family routine (as in the walk-to-school ritual or routine in Chapter 3). In Chapter 2, I discuss the use of question and answer sequences as a type of routine that engages children and raises the interactional relationship of the single parent family. Explicit talk about family membership or roles (as well as family members' histories and competencies) is another way that families "do" kinship (Chapters 3 and 4). In Chapter 5, I provide an overview of themes and phenomena in LGBTQ+ multilingual families—from gendered language use across languages to the intersections of sexuality with ethnolinguistic identities in relation to multilingualism as LGBTQ+ parents report the constraints and affordances of different languages in their home language use.

Kinship as action, as caregiving, as naming, and as languaging has implications for the study of multilingual families both in outcomes-based and in experience-based approaches to multilingual family studies. On the one hand, different family configurations, in terms of number of family members (specifically adult caregivers), have implications for the types of interactions children engage in and their bilingual outcomes. The possibilities for kinship relationships shape the interactional processes and possibilities for multilingualism at home. Related to this, the more complex processes of doing family—that is, negotiating relationships, roles, and values—require greater attention to the external worlds of children and adults as well as closer examination of the negotiations of power, cultural norms, and identities at home. From this point of view, the family can be a place of cultural transformation where children and parents disagree or strategically negotiate practices, routines, and languages (Fogle, 2012; Gafaranga, 2010; Said and Zhu Hua, 2017). While many studies in family language policy have discussed children's agency in the family and the resultant language shifts that children actively negotiate, there is little discussion about how these negotiations are tied to relationships with their parents, their external worlds, and the overall process of building a certain type of (bi- or multilingual) family. Studies that can examine these processes through more in-depth study, more careful consideration of caregiving (across contexts and modalities), gender and sexuality, and the external discourse environment can provide greater depth of examination into multilingual families.

The Studies and Methodological Approaches

All of the studies in this volume, despite their different participants, methods, and foci, are aimed at understanding the construction of kinship in relation to bi- and multilingualism in the family. That is, how do family construction, membership, and negotiation include or exclude the multilingual resources available to family members or the multilingual identities possible? This volume explores these questions from multiple perspectives in different contexts to bring together public, private, and public-private (e.g., research interview) constructions of multilingual (or monolingual) families. In all of these studies, I take the point of view that bi- or multilingualism is a social construct that can be displayed, enacted, and strategically employed in context and situated interaction (Lo and Kim, 2011; Otsuji and Pennycook, 2010; Wright, 2017, 2018).

There are three main approaches to family language that have informed the studies in this book: language socialization, family discourse, and family language policy. These different approaches work together at times to yield investigations of family ideologies, routines, and discourse and contribute to these areas by lending a non-normative, multilingual lens.

Language Socialization

First, work in language socialization that views parent/child, expert/novice interaction as a site of language learning and culture learning has provided a guiding framework for the interactional studies in this book that examine both adoptive and single parent families (Chapters 2, 3, and 4). There are many good reviews of the main theories, methods, and findings of language socialization studies (Garrett, 2008; Ochs and Schieffelin, 2011) that discuss how specific patterns of language use are tied to children's language development and acquisition of sociocultural norms. Language socialization research examines routines and patterns that, in early work, were seen as culture-specific, but from a more individualized perspective could also be family-specific (Fogle, 2012). Routines provide a scaffold for children's participation and development, and, in the case of some families, negotiation and resistance. Chapters 2 and 3 use a language socialization approach to identify a pattern of language use in one adoptive family, the use of questions, and a routine walk-to-school activity that frames Russian-English bilingual language use for a mother-daughter dyad.

Family Discourse

Family discourse is a second field of study that focuses on family interaction, mostly in monolingual families, to better understand how family identities and relationships are constructed in everyday discourse. Here the focus is not primarily on routine interactions and patterns over time, but rather types of talk (e.g., talk about the family or family members) and the discursive constructions of family and family identities in that talk. This work provides very clear data showing how families become certain types of families in talk (Kendall, 2007), how family members are constructed, and how family identities move across contexts in and out of the home (Gordon et al., 2007). Further, Tannen (2007) has made the very important point that discursive moves in family interaction are often multidimensional and can simultaneously signify solidarity and distance. This more nuanced and complex approach to family interaction allows for a deeper understanding of processes such as code-switching or translanguaging in multilingual families. Lanza's (1997/2004) early studies of family bilingualism drew on both language socialization and family discourse studies to demonstrate how specific interactional strategies influenced children's bilingual language development. I employ discourse analytic approaches to family conversations most specifically in Chapters 2, 3, and 4 where I examine conversations and parental strategies in single and adoptive parent families, but the analysis of interview and media data in the other chapters is also closely aligned with these constructivist approaches (Chapters 5 and 6).

Family Language Policy

Finally, as discussed above, family language policy grew out of an attempt to bring together the discursive and linguistic anthropological approaches to family language discussed above with the psycholinguistic research being conducted in the field of bilingual parenting and bilingual first language acquisition. Family language policy research has relied on both interview and interactional data (Fogle, 2012; King and Fogle, 2006), but interview data have typically been used to explore parents' language ideologies and connections between ideologies, practice, and planning in this field (Curdt-Christiansen, 2013; King and Fogle, 2006). In this volume, I examine interview data from different sets of parents for two main goals. In Chapter 2, I look at how single parents talk about their children in interviews to better understand how a collective parent-child identity is constructed in relation to decision-making processes in the family (i.e., how children achieve agency in single parent interviews). In Chapter 3, I look at a narrative excerpt with an adoptive mother to show how she constructs her children's competencies (that are unknown to her because they do not yet speak English) and herself as a good mother. These data and analyses expand on my previous work on parental ethnotheories to demonstrate the fact that language ideologies are embedded in larger understandings of family and childhood (Fogle, 2013a; Kulick, 1997).

Finally, there have been numerous calls in recent years to more carefully examine family external influences on family internal language policies (Canagarajah, 2008; King and Fogle, 2017; Macalister and Miravahedi, 2017); however, there is little discussion in the literature about how to examine discourses that are located outside of the family. Two chapters in this volume provide analyses of public discourse in the form of a media discourse analysis and a discussion of published works (documentaries, performance, and memoirs). The inclusion of public discourse constructions of kinship and family is rooted in Scollon and Scollon's (2004) assertion that language and social action needed to be studied simultaneously from three dimensions: the historical bodies of speakers, the interactional order of the local context, and the discourses in place that circulate from one action and one site to another. Most studies of family language focus on only one area of these three—usually either historical bodies instantiated in language ideologies and interview data or the interaction order analyzed through micro-analysis of family interaction. While the chapters in this book do not represent an ethnographic nexus analysis as laid out by Scollon and Scollon, the investigation of the construction of family in these different types of discourse was inspired by the nexus analysis approach.

In Chapter 2, I look at the strategic use of family reference (cf. Sclafani, 2015) and kinship terms in newspaper articles about Melania Trump's parents' citizenship ceremony to show how a monolingual, nuclear family is constructed in immigration debates. In the final chapter, I further examine public figures' and authors' own stances toward being queer and bilingual or members of bilingual families. In short, this volume offers ways of looking at kinship in relation to multilingualism in the family to demonstrate how kinships are constructed in interviews, family interactions, and public discourse and how such constructions rely on multilingual resources and identities.

Researcher Positionality

In a discussion about researcher positionality in the field of language policy and planning, Angel Lin (2015: 23) suggests, following Habermas (1979, 1987), that there are three "human interests" that underlie research and the production of knowledge. The first, according to Lin, can be considered positivist and aimed at outcomes (that can be readily consumed by policymakers, for example), the second is interpretative, that is, more descriptive and aimed at understanding or explaining cause-effect relationships (e.g., ethnography), and the third is critical and related to self-knowledge and transformation. Most of the studies in this book draw on positivist and interpretive methodologies that are aimed to identify and explain practices and routes to childhood bilingualism (or that was the original goal). As an undergraduate English literature major in the 1990s, however, I received a heavy amount of training in critical theory and critical approaches to literary criticism (that, as I understood it, focused on the critique of power structures and relations in fiction and other literary work). This study influenced the work I assumed would be "publishable" and "legitimate" in the world of applied linguistics, where critical approaches did not seem to have the same value (Pennycook, 2001).

While the humanities and other areas of social sciences (e.g., anthropology) have begun to move away from critical theory (to post-humanist, embodied, and even empirical approaches), kinship studies and family language studies can benefit from the kind of reflexive, transformative examination critical approaches bring in order to not only accept and incorporate new definitions of "family" but also center discourse as means for understanding family language processes. As Lin notes, "adopting a critical stance is very important if Language Policy and Planning research is to contribute to promoting social justice and challenging unequal relations of power often found in LPP contexts" (p. 30). My goal is to bring to the foreground the families that have been left out of family language studies and show why considering them is integral to understanding all family language processes.

The analyses in these chapters are largely qualitative (with the exception of Chapter 2), and some are part of larger, ethnographic case studies of families (Fogle, 2012). I have written about my relationship to these families and my role as researcher briefly in the original publications from which these studies are taken. However, as I have matured as a researcher and watched my own research agenda unfold, it has become clearer to me how my own private life, personal decisions, and stance toward family life have shaped my perspective on research on multilingual families and the types of questions I have begun to ask.

In an interview on the popular radio program *On Being* ("Jane Berko Gleason–Unfolding Language, Unfolding Life," n.d.), well-known child language researcher Jane Berko Gleason noted that parents make the best researchers of child language because they know first-hand how children produce language and are better interpreters of children's behaviors, and this may in fact be true as her early studies demonstrated that mothers (who at the time stayed at home with young children) had better understanding than fathers of children's language production (1975). The problem with being a parent researcher, however, as with any in-group/out-group positionality, is that one becomes blindsided by one's own in-group membership or one's own situation and tends to exclude other possibilities. I believe this has happened in family language research as researchers have sought participants who are "convenient" or comfortable and not rigorously applied selection criteria to their studies (although it can be difficult to recruit diverse families as I discuss in the final chapter). While the field of multilingual families is expanding, and more and more diverse families are studied, there is still little discussion of what a family is and why the family itself matters despite the opportunities diverse families open up for exploring these questions.

As a researcher-parent, my own family has seen enormous changes since the birth of my one son in 2007. At that time, I was working on my dissertation in Washington, DC. I was married to a cisgender man, and we had no extended family around us. We were very much like the dual-career families documented in Ochs and Kremer-Sedlik's (2013) volume on postindustrial parenting—extremely busy, achievement-oriented, and accommodating to our child. Unlike the families in that book (or ideologically like those families perhaps), we relied on a paid caregiver to create a Russian language immersion environment in our home to promote additive bilingualism for our child.

Eight months after my son's birth, I started commuting to New York from Washington, DC, for my first academic job. During that year, I began to question my bisexual identity for a second major time in my life (I came out the first time when I was eighteen). In an effort to pursue my academic career and to keep my marriage together, my then husband and I moved to Mississippi where I had the opportunity to work with some wonderful colleagues at Mississippi State University. My son largely lost contact with Russian speakers in Mississippi. After a while, he started to tell me to stop speaking "Spanish" when I spoke to him in Russian, inserting local language ideologies into our home interactions (despite the fact that Mississippi is a multilingual place [cf. Wright, 2018]).

Four years later, my husband and I decided to divorce and establish a co-parenting relationship in different cities in the South. I had primary custody of my son, and he saw his father twice a month. I came out more publicly as queer and began dating women. My ex-husband and I used technology and frequent road trips to keep our son connected. And while the studies in this volume do not capture such digital, mobile parenting, there are other researchers working on this in relation to multilingualism and single parent and extended, transnational families (Palviainen, 2020; Lexander and Androstopoulous, 2019). During this time, I conducted a study of Russian-speaking mothers in the Southern United States, where my interest in single mothers began to develop as the mother in Chapter 3 had a very similar routine as I did with my son in walking to school every morning except that she spoke Russian during that time (and here my focus on that family was of interest because of the similarity to my own). I also began to explore connections between sexual fluidity and linguistic fluidity and experiment with different types of analysis and texts (as working in English departments afforded more interdisciplinarity in my work), specifically works of fiction (Wright, 2018). I continue to look for ways to include diverse voices and texts in my work as represented in this volume where I include literary memoir, documentary, and media discourse in Chapters 5 and 6.

Four years into single parenting at the time of writing, my son has finished elementary school and has started middle school this year. He has the opportunity to learn Russian at the new school and for months has been asking me how to say things in Russian and to speak Russian with him. My own online dating life, where I have met Russian speakers and have begun to use Russian more as a part of my daily repertoire, as well as my research activities where I form acquaintances with Russian-speaking research assistants and participants, has improved my own Russian competence and opportunities for contact in Russian-speaking regions. Parental divorce, dating, and mobility open children's worlds to more potential adult friends and caregivers and expand the linguistic network of the family, so to speak. These are aspects of family life that are not usually captured in discussions of single and LGBTQ+ parenting or by the research models employed in family language research.

My parenting, my family, my online dating life, and my research are all closely intertwined. I think perhaps this is the point that the famous psychologist Roger Brown (1996) tried to make when he published the memoir of his sex life with his partner at the end of his career in the title of which he refers to himself as an "eminent *gay* psychologist" (emphasis mine)—we are people first even if our research community does not always see or hear us, and our personal experiences influence our research interests and perspectives. Being a queer-identified, single mother greatly shifted the research I was interested in and wanted to do. Who were we studying and why? Why was the field of applied linguistics so normative, and why did studies of family language policy seem to indicate there was only one type of family in the world? For multilingual, transnational families perhaps one of the most important aspects of life linguists can study is how to negotiate new genders, relationships, and family configurations in relation to language—these social transformations have real consequences for transmigrant adults and children both in and out of educational settings. For my own family, shifts in the household, my contact and relationships with speakers of Russian, and mobility have influenced my son's desire and opportunities to learn Russian even if he does not see those processes at work around him.

From Outcomes to Experiences

In this volume, I present critical multilingual family language studies that aim to uncover the linguistic practices and actions that construct kinships through discursive analysis in and with bi- and multilingual families. This approach mandates a focus on diverse families where kinship relations and roles are negotiated and constructed through language, for example, the single parent, adoptive, and LGBTQ+-identified families discussed in this volume along with transnational, extended, child-headed, blended, and other diverse family configurations. Such families bring kinship to the foreground as a way of contextualizing multilingual language experiences in the family and demonstrate how family construction influences language use and, potentially, development. This book specifically examines why single parents have been found to be successful at raising bilingual children through analyses of how they talk about and to their children (Chapter 2), how a routine activity (walking to school) and mother-daughter bonding intersect with minority language use (Chapter 3), how adoptive parents uncover children's hidden histories and competencies in the context of multilingual pasts (Chapter 4), how LGBTQ+-identified families negotiate inclusion and exclusion through bi- and multilingual language use (Chapter 5), and how monolingual normativity is constructed in relation to the nuclear family in coverage of the Trump family (Chapter 6). Practice-based approaches to kinship that focus on inclusion and exclusion as well as caregiving relationships inform these analyses to show how multilingualism shapes and is shaped by family roles and relationships. By taking family first and decentering the normative, nuclear family, this volume offers new data and analyses that embed language in kinship, gender and sexuality, and the construction of care. The final chapter further provides suggestions for creating more ethical and inclusive research design in the study of multilingual family language and connects the family-as-construct approach to other contexts such as the school.

By centering minority families (single parent, adoptive, and LGBTQ+) within the minority of bi- and multilingual families in the contexts in which the participants in these studies are situated, this book pushes boundaries in the field of family language studies by arguing that it is family formation and kinship processes that account for language use, including bi- and multilingualism in the family. Kinship processes form an intermediary link that integrates family external discourses and representations of language in the family, children's experiences across time and space, and the interactional patterns of everyday language use in the family. The book considers the family as both a context for development and an active construct that is negotiated in interaction, and provides insight into how to bring together both positivist outcome-oriented and more interpretive experience-oriented approaches to understanding family multilingualism. Crucially, the studies in this volume show that examining family configuration and kinship building together can lead to new understandings of the interactional, ideological, and affective factors that lead to bi- and multilingual outcomes for children as well as how bi- and multilingualism play a role in family formation and kinship.

2

Why Are Single Parents Good at Using a Minority Language?: Talking about and to Kids

In a study of the language input and bilingual outcome patterns of 1,899 bilingual families in the Netherlands, De Houwer (2007) found that single parents were potentially better at raising bilingual children because use of the minority language was a "defining feature" of family communication (p. 415). In my own research, single parents have reported greater use of minority languages at home (for example, one single adoptive father took intensive Russian classes at a local university before adopting his two sons from Ukraine) and greater satisfaction with their children's bilingualism in comparison to dual parent families as I discuss below in this chapter and in Chapter 3. However, there are very few studies of single parents, both monolingual and multilingual, in family language research despite the potential linguistic advantages of growing up in a single parent family and a wealth of research in other fields on single parenting such as clinical psychology, literacy, and child development that have examined differences in family configuration (cf. Lansford et al., 2001).

The omission of single parent families presents an ethically problematic gap in the research on bi- and multilingual parenting and family language more generally that not only excludes a large number of families from the research and limits the generalizability or application of findings to only one type of family, but also obscures possible theoretical issues such as family configuration (adult-child ratios) and family relationships (including children's agency and collaboration in interactional events). Single parents have been found to engage in family construction projects in interaction and bond with children in different ways from dual parent families. These processes shed light on kinship and family role formation in the single parent family and how language practices play a role in constructing the linguistic environment of the single parent home, the connections and kinships single parents rely on outside of the home for extended caregiving and support, and the collaboration between parent and children in decision making and identity construction. As a first step, this chapter offers two main potential ways (in relation to how single parents talk to their children and about their children) in which single parents, both monolingual and multilingual, differ from partnered parents in the interactional strategies they use at home and ideological orientations toward children as communication partners and family members.

If the goal in family language policy and multilingual parenting research is to examine what language ideologies and practices lead to bilingual outcomes for children, single parent families offer perspectives on success. If the goal is rather (as discussed in Chapter 1) how individual family members experience multilingualism in the family (Zhu Hua and Li Wei, 2016), examining single parent multilingual families is essential to understanding the role of minority languages in parent-child relationships and kinship processes. Single parents who use the minority language "by default" do so perhaps not only as a way of maintaining their own linguistic identities, but in collaboration with children also as a way to establish a family identity, belonging, and heritage connection that can be harder to achieve when parents speak different first languages or the minority language relationship between the parents does not easily extend to children (i.e., the parents use the L1 together but find it easier to use the L2 with children).

Family interaction is complex—structural, ideological, and emotional differences among single parent and dual parent families play a role in the differences in bilingual language use and outcomes (and every family is different, as Zhu Hua and Li Wei [2016] point out). In this chapter and the following chapter (Chapter 3), I explore how the family configuration of a single parent home affects the interactional environment of the child(ren) from a context-based or outcomes-based approach as discussed above and also examine how differences in the parent-child relationship in single parent families also influence minority language use and the construction of multilingual family histories and identities. In short, these two chapters point to a need for greater understanding of multilingual single parent language use as a key to understanding effective strategies and the family-based experiences that lead to maintaining heritage or minority languages at home.

Understanding Single Parent Families

Single parent families are formed in a variety of ways—by choice, by divorce, or by circumstance—and have historically been scapegoated as an indicator of social problems and cause of educational and emotional deficits for children, specifically in the US context (Coontz, 2016). However, single parent families are not uncommon, recent reports suggest that 24 percent of families in the United States are headed by a single mother (Mather, 2010) and single parent households make up about 15 percent of all families worldwide (OECD, 2011). In fact, more mothers are choosing to have children on their own without a partner through reproductive technologies and changing the face of single parenthood. Research on single parents and single parent families has found that while some children struggle after divorce, many of the discrepancies in educational and emotional outcomes are attributable to socioeconomic status and financial issues that single mothers in particular face. Single parents at higher socioeconomic status raise children who are as successful as dual parent families and may in some cases have greater competence in some areas (Coontz, 2016). That is, there is nothing inherently dangerous or deleterious for children raised in a single parent family. However, the stress placed on single parents by work instability or systemic inequities (lack of before- and after-school care, inflexible work schedules, or financial stress) can affect both single parents and subsequently their children negatively. For bilingual single parents, the same is potentially true—single parents who are financially and socially secure may create an optimal environment for bi- and multilingual development, while those who experience stress and financial insecurity and do not have strong social support networks might find negotiating bilingualism more challenging.

Bilingual Single Parents

In outcomes-based (family-as-context) studies of bilingual parenting, it has been noted that single parents may be more effective than partnered parents at maintaining minority languages at home. De Houwer (2007: 415) referred to the single parent's minority language use as a "defining feature" of communication for single parented households. In her study of parental input patterns with 1,899 parents (121 single parent families) in the Netherlands who were bilingual in Dutch and another language, De Houwer found that 38 percent of single parents reported using only the minority language at home as compared to 11 percent of dual parent families. In addition, the overall percentage of children who spoke only Dutch (and not the parents' home or minority language) was lower in single parent families (15.7 percent) than in dual parent families (23.85 percent). These findings, as De Houwer noted, suggest that single parents may be more successful at maintaining a minority language at home, but there are very few studies that followed up with focused examination of these differences or included single parent families in multilingual family research.

Furthermore, the reasons for these differences are not immediately apparent and require a qualitative approach to understanding how single parents interact with their children and why they might be more impervious to children's so-called medium requests in interaction (Gafaranga, 2010) or why children themselves might be less likely to resist the parent's preferred language. The analyses in this chapter of how single parents in multilingual contexts talk to their children and about their children provide some avenues for further research in understanding the interactional and ideological differences of single parent families. In the following chapter, I examine more closely the forging of a bilingual single mother-daughter relationship.

Other researchers interested in family bilingualism have also noted that single parents are effective at raising bilingual children. In 2010, Obied published a paper titled "Can One-Parent Families or Divorced Families Produce Two-Language Children? An Investigation into How Portuguese–English Bilingual Children Acquire Biliteracy within Diverse Family Structures." The title alone pointed to major biases in the study of bilingual parenting and family language policy—that research to that date had assumed a two-parent norm and additionally drawn on "one-parent-one-language" ideology that suggested the elitist notion that bilingual children must be raised by two parents speaking two different languages (Döpke, 1998). Obied's study noted the bias in bilingual parenting research against single parents, including an underlying belief that single parents are overly stressed and unable to provide the linguistic environment for bilingual development (that is clearly refuted by De Houwer's [2007] findings). As Obied (2010: 227) noted:

> Previous research has either ignored bilingual children growing up in diverse family structures, or presented these families negatively in terms of children developing biliteracy.

In her study of Portuguese-English bilingual single parent families in Portugal, Obied found that single parents provided community networks, siblings contributed to minority language use, and that a non-residential parent could also help with biliteracy development in single parent families. This study points to the ways in which varied kinships for the child (with siblings, community members, and parents who live in a different household) entail diverse language competencies and repertoires.

The context of single motherhood and multilingualism can play a role in the sense of success or satisfaction with children's bilingualism. Macalister and Navarro (2016) examined how the stressors of being a refugee migrant mother in New Zealand affected both the learning of English and maintenance of Spanish at home. This study focused on two single mother refugees who were enrolled in an adult ESOL program and participated in ethnographic interviews over a period of eighteen months. Like in De Houwer's and Obied's studies, Navarro and Macalister noted that "the mothers tended to use Spanish with their children, [but] the children demonstrated greater facility in switching languages depending on who they were interacting with, and where" (p. 126). The single mothers in this study reported feeling strapped for time and resources and unable to help their children with English language homework and school tasks because of their own limited educational background. However, there is evidence in the data that the children were proficient speakers of Spanish and, for the most part, able to succeed in the English medium school (except perhaps for one participant who preferred

Spanish). So in relation to raising bilingual children, which was not the sole focus of the analysis in the study, the single mothers did seem successful. Closer consideration of the family relationships and identities of the children could relate to the language-related findings in this study, especially for the one child participant who preferred Spanish and had a difficult time learning English at school.

The studies reviewed above show that single mothers in particular choose to use their first language or minority language with their children and potentially construct networks that support minority language use. In the following family language studies, single parents have also been found to involve their children in joint decision making and afford children agency in interaction. In a multi-year language socialization study of five families of single parents by choice (i.e., mothers who formed families through adoption or reproductive technologies with no partner) in Spain, Poveda et al. (2014) noted that single mothers held three socialization goals that are different from dual parent families: (a) the mother-child dyad is not defined by the absence of a father and social networks are involved in caregiving (including other single parent families), (b) single mothers are reflexive and concerned about children's agency and role in the family, and (c) single mothers have policies of open disclosure and talk about their children's origins (p. 323). By eschewing a two-parent model and deficit approaches to single parenting (i.e., that compare single parent families in relation to dual parent families), Poveda et al. were able to demonstrate how children were involved in co-constructing their roles in the family and family identities as well as how the single parent family was enmeshed in a network of other families and social relations in everyday interactions that involved talking about current and future events. While children in dual parent families undoubtedly take part in such conversations, the family formation processes may not be as transparent as they are in single parent families (where a mother must explain how a child was conceived in absence of a father, for example). Studying single parent families highlights the importance of these family building projects for children and connects to other aspects of family language such as the interactional strategies used by parents to engage children in conversation and the use of a minority language, which will be discussed in greater detail in relation to the data presented here.

The emergence of children's agency in the single parent family is also found in contexts of transmigration. Gallo and Hornberger (2019), using an ethnography of language policy and planning approach, examine the language ideologies and practices in one young Mexican American girl's family after her father's deportation to Mexico. Through observation and recordings at school and home, the authors demonstrated that the family language policy changed in response to the family's changing migratory futures (i.e., to return to Mexico or stay in the United States), and that the daughter Princess played an active role in making both language and migration decisions with her mother. Deportation of Princess's father left her mother as a single mom with two children, a change in the family configuration that led to interactional differences at home, according to the study:

> After her husband's deportation, Cinthia commented on how she felt like she now talked to eight-year-old Princess like an adult, no longer like *una niña* (a little girl). As Cinthia navigated difficult decisions regarding her family's life in Mexico or the USA, she engaged Princess in these conversations and decisions, and through her talk Princess actively contributed to family migration decisions. (p. 766)

For Princess, the deportation of her father had clear implications for her own language learning as the need to learn Spanish, and particularly Spanish literacy, increased in response to the possible move to Mexico to reunite the family. The changes in family structure as a result of deportation led to Princess taking a more active role in family language policy processes.

Single parenting is not necessarily one-adult caregiving. Coetzee (2018) explored another context of single motherhood, specifically in the South African context where adolescent mothers raise children with the help of extended family members (grandmothers, aunts, and non-residential fathers). Coetzee's study demonstrated not only how children acquired different language competencies outside of the nuclear family, but also, more interestingly, how extended family members engaged in and were implicated in children's acquisition of taboo language in specific. The use of taboo language (swearing) was associated with the use of a certain code (Afrikaans rather than English), and further the caregivers in the study did not take direct responsibility for teaching the swear words to young children. In the case of one boy (an infant), for example, both the mother and the father blamed each other for teaching the child taboo language (even though the child was pre-verbal and utterances were interpreted by adults). Coetzee's examination demonstrates how family internal and family external socialization depend on a nuclear family norm where two parents are seen as responsible for family language policy when in fact many caregivers with contradictory intentions and practices could be at play across time and space—complicating where family is located and who is responsible for family language policies.

From an outcomes-based approach, single parents are potentially better at maintaining minority languages because there is no other adult language in the home, they build minority language communities that facilitate childcare outside of the home, and they use other modalities to stay connected to non-residential co-parents. From an experience-based or family-as-construct approach, the single parent family avoids power struggles and gender norms of the dual-parented, cisgender, heterosexual families that are potentially tied to language negotiations in the family. Single parents are also known to accommodate to children more and include them in joint decision-making processes. Therefore, if the desire is to know how to promote a minority language at home, the answer might be to look to single parents.

Chapter Overview

In an effort to understand the potential differences in single parent family interactions as well as single parents' perspectives on family relationships and the role of children in the family based on the above discussions, this chapter examines interactional and interview data from three studies of parents in bilingual contexts (i.e., transnational adoptive families or bilingual parents) and compares single parents to married/partnered parents in the language strategies they use at home and the ways in which they talk about their children in interviews. The goal of these analyses is to show that single parents in these studies had very different alignments to their children and interactional strategies in conversation than partnered parents. While the data do not directly show that single parents are better at maintaining a minority language at home (because the adoptive families were monolingual English-speaking families at the time of the data collection), the findings do show that interactional and discursive patterns are different in the two different family configurations. The ways in which these differences can explain bilingual development patterns for children in single parent families will be discussed further in Chapter 3 in a closer examination of Russian language use in a single parent family.

The first part of the chapter turns to a reanalysis of some data collected for the Fogle (2012) study of adoptive parents of Russian-speaking regions (Study 1). In this analysis, I show that the single father in one family asked significantly more questions than the partnered parents in another family in mealtime conversations. The second part of the analysis examines interview data from adoptive parents (Fogle, 2013a) (Study 2) and Russian-speaking mothers (Study 3) to demonstrate how single parents involve their children as joint decision makers and collaborators in the family.

How Single Parents Talk *to* Their Children

Structural differences in the single parent family make children the exclusive conversation partner(s) to the single adult. On the one hand, this structural configuration requires children to be "raised" to the parent's discursive level because the child fills the place, so to speak, of an adult partner. On the other hand, this configuration can also lead to greater parent accommodation to the child, specifically in relation to joint decision making and collaboration (Poveda et al., 2014) (see also Ochs and Schieffelin, 1984 for a discussion of child raising/self-lowering). In the data presented here, this dual process is apparent as the single adoptive parent (with two sons from Ukraine who speak English) uses an interactive strategy that constructs the boys as equal interactants through the use of repeated questions designed to raise the level of conversation while at the same time represents greater accommodation to the children's experiences, needs, and desires by querying their perspectives and thoughts. In the following section, I compare the single father's (John's) and his sons' frequency of question use in mealtime conversations to a second adoptive family's frequency of use. I find an inverse relationship with John using about the same number of questions as the children in the second family. I argue that these patterns can be understood in relation to the parenting configuration and differences between single and partnered parents.

Methods

Two families participated in the study from which these data are taken (Fogle, 2012). The study was a longitudinal, language socialization study of culture and language in the transnational (Russia) adoptive family. The first family (Family 1), the Sondermanns, was made up of a single father and two boys adopted from Ukraine about a year prior to the start of the study. The father John was a psychotherapist, he had taken two semesters of intensive Russian to communicate with his children prior to the adoption, and he had a strong focus on literacy learning at home. Both boys, Dima and Sasha, were dominant in English at the time of the study and were doing well in school. The second family (Family 2), the Jackson-Wessels, was made up of a mother, father, and two children. Kevin was a stay-at-home father and was homeschooling the two children at the time of the study. The parents in this family did not speak Russian, and the children had not maintained contact with Russian. Kevin focused on literacy and play in his instruction with the children during the day. The children, Arkadiy and Anna, were fluent in English but had a high degree of idiosyncratic grammatical forms. They also asked a lot of questions (similar to younger children in first-language acquisition contexts), which the parents commented on and is the focus on the following analysis. The parents in both families held graduate degrees, and the fathers were the primary caregivers. John's children, Dima and Sasha, were nine and eight at the time of recording. Kevin and Melissa's children, Arkadiy and Anna, were six and four.

For this study, three mealtime recordings (self-recorded by the parents) over the first three months of data collection (in 2007) were selected at random for analysis (87 minutes in John's family; 53 minutes in Kevin's family). These conversations were transcribed using the CHILDES conventions and verified by a second transcriber.

Questions in these data were determined by syntactic formation (use of inversion or wh-element) as well as rising intonation (as determined by the transcribers). Six exhaustive and mutually exclusive question types were identified through emic analysis of the data. These were coded using CHILDES. For the current analysis, however, these six question types were considered as two larger categories: prompts and reactive questions. Prompting questions were defined as interrogatives used to elicit talk from one or more speakers that do not react directly to a prior utterance. These included attention getters, initiations of a new topic, and prompts for elaboration on same topic. Reactive questions were interrogatives used to target another speaker's utterance. These questions served to clarify, correct, confirm, or elicit more information. Reactive questions included responses to actions (e.g., misbehavior) and repetitions of questions.

Interrater reliability on 10 percent of the data was established for the interrogative categories defined above (Cohen's Kappa = .84) and differences were discussed and resolved by the raters. Fourteen questions were omitted from the analysis because they were issued by a parent to a parent in Family 2 and no such comparable forms were available in Family 1.

Overall, the two families together produced 3,891 utterances and 728 questions in the three mealtime recordings. In the combined data, about 19 percent of all utterances were questions. The most common category of question for all speakers was reactive (i.e., questions responding to a prior utterance). Chi-square tests were applied to the data to determine if predictable patterns in question use existed in the two families.

Question Use Patterns

Reverse trends in question use were found in the two families as can be seen in Table 2.1. In Family 1 (John), the father was more likely to use questions than the parents in Family 2 (Kevin). In the family conversations, 29.6 percent of all of the father John's utterances in Family 1 were questions while only 11.2 percent of all of Kevin and Meredith's utterances combined were questions in Family 2. In contrast, the children in Family 2 produced questions about 25.5 percent of the time while the children in Family 1 used about 11.4 percent of questions. So the single father in Family 1 asked the about same percentage of all questions as the children in Family 2, and the married parents in Family 2 asked the same percentage of questions as the children in Family 1 as seen in the Figure 2.1.

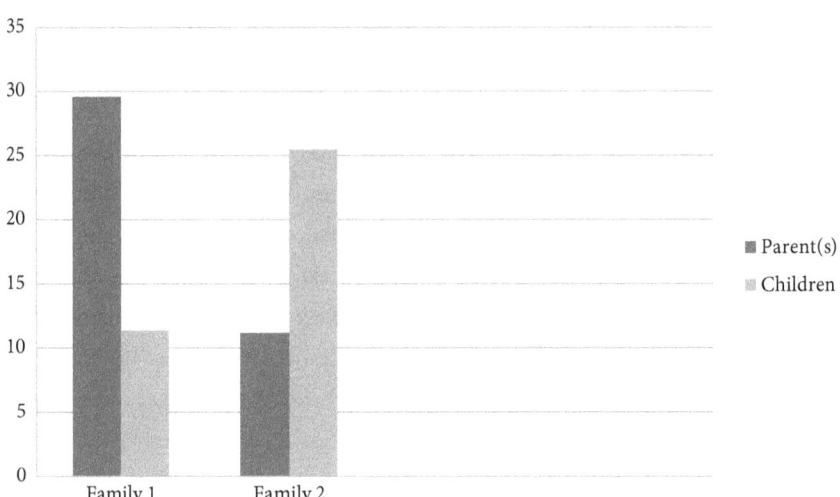

Figure 2.1 Percentage of Questions.

According to the chi-square tests, these findings were significant (Parents: $\chi^2 = 9.18$, $p < .05$; Children: $\chi^2 = 7.33$, $p < .05$), and a predictable pattern of question use was found in the two families. In terms of question type, that is, prompting vs. reactive, no significant differences were found for the parents across families. On the whole, 44 percent of all questions were prompts for John in Family 1 and 34 percent for Kevin and Meredith in Family 2.

The pattern of question types in the children's discourse across the two families, however, was significant. The children in Family 2 were more likely to produce prompting-type questions, while the children in Family 1 were more likely to produce reactive questions. Overall, 66 percent of Arkadiy's and Anna's questions were prompts whereas 44 percent of Dima's and Sasha's questions were prompts. In sum, then, the analysis of question use showed that in Family 1, the father was more likely to question his children. In Family 2, the children were more likely to question their parents. Furthermore, Arkadiy and Anna (Family 2) were more likely to use prompts than the children in Family 1 to introduce new topics in the conversation.

These patterns are evident in the following excerpts from the family conversations. In Excerpt 2.1, John prompts Sasha (the younger child) to talk about activities at their friends' house (John frequently worked late, and the boys stayed with other caregivers in the evenings as discussed in other studies of single parents above). Dima, the older child, responds that they were doing "nothing" (cf. Fogle, 2012), while Sasha provides an explanatory response about playing Jenga, a popular wooden block-building game.

Excerpt 2.1 Family 1 questions
(Study 1; December 2005)
Transcribed using CHAT conventions (MacWhinney, 2000)

1	**John:**	**So Sasha what were you doing in Kate and Jen's?**
2	Dima:	Nothing.
3	Sasha:	Ah building towers with +...
4	**John:**	**building towers?**
5	Sasha:	Uh huh.
6	**John:**	**With what?**
7	Sasha:	With # these # blo:cks
8	John:	mmhmm
9	Sasha:	not uh - uh - like we have # those flat and uh xx +...
10	Dima:	Jenga.
11	Sasha:	[Yeah.]
12	Dima:	[janga] janga janga janga!

In this short excerpt, three of John's utterances are questions (in bold)—one initiatory to elicit talk from Sasha, two reactive to scaffold Sasha's production. John uses questions in this excerpt to target a trouble spot (i.e., Sasha's inability to remember the name of the blocks) and push Sasha to complete his thought. By prompting the children in this way to talk about a specific topic and event and then following up with reactive, scaffolding strategies, John selects the speaker, the format, and the content of the conversation. This strategy was more successful with the younger child than the older child Dima, however. John's question use was tied to his own perception of his role as a facilitator of the children's language development as he noted in interviews. This use is potentially also tied to his professional training as a therapist in which asking questions is an important aspect of talk therapy. However, as a single parent the question use scaffolds the children into "adult" conversation and allows Sasha in this case to become an equal interactional partner.

In Family 2, the interactions between parents and children and the patterns in the use of questions are very different as found in the quantitative analysis. In the following excerpt in which the family is talking about the Thanksgiving dinner leftovers they are eating, Anna and Arkadiy use a number of questions and attention-getters to interrupt the conversation:

Excerpt 2.2 Family 2 questions
(Study 1; November 2005)

1	Meredith:	Anna use a fork.
2		Uhm- we'll take - # once it's
3	Anna:	What is this?
4	Kevin:	Corn.
5		Come on, eat.
6	Anna:	[What]?
7	Arkadiy:	[Mama]?
8	Kevin:	Just eat little girl.
9	Anna:	xxx.
10	Arkadiy:	Mama?
11		What kind number is December?
12	Meredith:	December is the last month of the year.
13	Kevin:	The month twelve.
14	Meredith:	And # the calendar there is to count down how many days [from the first day of Decem-]
15	Anna:	[Remember we went]
16	Meredith:	I - I'm talking right now.

All of Anna's and Arkadiy's contributions in the excerpt, except for possibly in Line 9, which was unintelligible, are questions. In Line 6, Anna begins a question, but does not finish because Arkadiy asks another question, and the two compete for the floor. The children's questions serve to engage the parents in conversation as well as to obtain information such as what food they are eating or what month December is. This information does get recycled in subsequent talk as seen in this excerpt four lines later.

Excerpt 2.3 Recycling of the word "corn"

1	Anna:	Mama mama?
2	Meredith:	Yes.
3	Anna:	You know what?
4		This is corn.
5	Meredith:	Yes.
6		I know that.

Here, we see that Anna uses the information obtained through her questioning strategies in order to engage her mother in subsequent turns as well as the use of two interrogative attention getters (Lines 1 and 3) to introduce the new topic.

The interactions in the two families differ as either parent-initiated or child-initiated. In Family 1, John nominates his children as speakers through the use of interrogative prompts. He identifies trouble spots and uses reactive interrogatives to elicit expansions from his children. And he uses these strategies to achieve larger discourse goals, such as having his children tell narratives about their day and promote "civil" discourse at the dinner table (as he noted in interviews). In the end, this causes Sasha and Dima to fit into a discourse framework established by their father and also puts the father in an accommodating position to the children as he anticipates their interactional needs and scaffolds their production.

In contrast, speakers and topics are often nominated by the children in Family 2, usually with an initiatory wh-question. The children also used information-seeking questions to obtain linguistic information such as the name of the food they are eating or more explanation about the parents' discourse. These strategies transfer the conversational burden off of the children and prompt parents to take longer "explanatory" turns. In this case, the children set the framework for family interactions and parents are placed in a responsive position. This pattern may be related to the fact that the parents held conversations that were "above the heads" of the children, and the children acted to find ways to take part in the family discussions. This approach also fit with Kevin's view of himself as a linguistic "model" (as contrasted to "facilitator") for the language-learning children (Fogle, 2012).

There are of course other factors that can explain the discourse patterns found in these two families. There is evidence to suggest that younger children issue more questions than older children (Smith, 1933), and Arkadiy and Anna in Family 2 are slightly younger than Dima and Sasha. However, this does not explain the older child Arkadiy's frequent use of questions, nor does it explain the father in Family 1's frequent question use in relation to the two other parents. Other explanations of these data might have to do with larger macro-level choices made by the parents. John's use of Russian in the first six months may have stemmed from a need for the children to develop questioning strategies because the children had access to the conversation in their native language. In addition, unlike John, Kevin, the father in Family 2, was more involved in his children's everyday activities and may have constrained the need for prompting stories about the day from the children at dinnertime.

While these two families were not able to maintain Russian as a language at home, the findings did suggest some major differences in single parent vs. dual parent family interactions. It is most likely not the case that all single parents use the same kind of questioning and scaffolding strategies that John did in his conversations with his children. However, single parents do serve as a more available and potentially active conversational partner to children. John's kids, for example, did not need to develop interrupting strategies to get the parents' attention because he did not have another adult interactant at home. The construction of an adult-child (vertical) conversational context in which the children were required to interact with their father in different ways than children in adult-adult, child-child (horizontal) configurations could shape bilingual language use and bilingual outcomes in active bilingual families. John's use of self-preservation strategies to raise the children's conversational level and scaffold talk could also apply in bilingual language use with a minority language-speaking parent. Scaffolding use of the minority language could be a way for a single parent to simply maintain their identity and balance at home. Furthermore, in keeping with Lanza's (1997/2004) work on discourse strategies of parents and work in second-language acquisition on teachers' use of questions, it may be that using more questions provides children more opportunity to produce language (as the children in Family 2 turned the conversational floor over to parents through the use of questions). For bi- and multilingual caregivers, this could mean more production in the minority language.

These processes are not only attributed to the structural aspects of the single parent configuration, but also related to the socialization processes in single parent families where children potentially achieve greater agency and are more conscious of their family status and roles within the family. In the following section, I focus on how single parents talk about their children in interviews to demonstrate that the parent-child alignments that emerge in John's family's data are present in other single parent families. Specifically, I focus on the use of "we" by single parents to include both themselves as parent and their children as active decision makers in the family in interviews.

How Single Parents Talk *about* Their Children

This section involves data from two interview studies with parents about their children's bilingualism and language learning. While the two groups of participants, adoptive parents of transnational adoptees and Russian-speaking mothers, were primarily made up of married parents, some single parents took part in these interviews (i.e., single parents were not actively recruited, and the data presented in this section are "incidental" [Fogle and King, 2014; Liddicoat, 2009]). As I conducted these interviews, it occurred to me that single parents spoke about their children and themselves differently than partnered or married parents. In specific, single parents were more likely to include children as decisions makers in the interview context or to construct an ambiguous "we" that involved children as partners in important events. Married and partnered parents in my interview data were more likely referred to "we" as the parents and other adult caregiver, but single parents used "we" to refer to themselves and the child(ren).

"We/They" in Discourse

Prior research in discourse analysis has pointed to the importance of pronominal use and reference in establishing collective vs. individual identities. In an analysis of Holocaust narratives that examined the construction of a mother-daughter relationship, Schiffrin (2002) demonstrated how one narrator constructed her family relationships in the discourse through shifting use of pronouns "we" and "they." Schiffrin concluded that the main narrator Ilse's use of "we" to refer to herself and her friends and consistent exclusion of her mother as a referent for "we" (i.e., that she never referred to herself and her mother together as "we") pointed to the isolation of Ilse from her family:

> The singularity of Ilse's mother is not only a stark contrast with the collective identity of Ilse's friends, but also a sharp reminder that although Ilse was embedded within a group of friends, the family that she could also have called we, was absent from her life story. (Schiffrin, 2002: 337)

Other studies have pointed to the exclusionary and inclusionary uses of "we" vs. "them" in constructing ethnic group identities (De Fina, 2003). Like Schiffrin's analysis of pronouns in the Holocaust narrative that construct different collective identities for the narrator, interview data from parents can be examined for the construction of collective family identities. In this section, I examine variation in the use of "we" to point to the ways in which child agency and joint decision making are constructed in interviews about family language policy.

Data and Methods

This section draws on data from two studies of language ideologies and family language policy, the first with adoptive parents (Fogle, 2013a) and the second with new data from Russian-speaking mothers in the United States. Table 2.1 shows the participant information for each of these studies.

Table 2.1 Interview Participants

Family configuration	Parent	Study	Education	# of children
Single	John	Adoptive	MA x2	2
	Lucy	Adoptive	MA	1
	Margaret	Adoptive	PhD	2
	Elena	Russian mothers	PhD	1
	Lena	Russian mothers	MBA	1

Family configuration	Parent	Study	Education	# of children
Partnered	Michelle	Adoptive	BA	2
	Jane	Adoptive	PhD	1
	Kevin	Adoptive	JD	2
	Laura	Russian mothers	BA	1
	Nicole	Russian mothers	BA	2

There were fewer single parent participants in both study groups. For the adoptive parents, only three parents identified as single at the time of the interview. John was a single father by choice, Lucy reported starting the adoption process with her husband but then got a divorce prior to adoption, and Margaret was also a single mother by choice but had a live-in partner at the time of the interview. For the Russian-speaking mothers, two mothers identified as single. Lena's husband had chosen not to move with Lena to the United States in the 1980s when she obtained refugee status, but her mother did live in the household. Second, Elena moved to the United States to do her graduate work before she had a child. Her child's father lived in Ukraine. Even among the group of "single parents," there was a great deal of diversity in relation to the role of additional family members and experiences leading up to the arrival of the child.

The partnered parents were selected at random in order to create a comparable data set to the five single participants. Across the two studies, a total of eighteen parents participated, eight of these were excluded from this study in order to compare single parents to partnered parents. All of the participants were parents of children who had Russian as a first or bilingual first language. Some of the parents in these groups were native English speakers (the adoptive parents) and some were native Russian speakers who chose to use either English or Russian in the interviews. Not all of the parents were bilingual. All of the data used for this study were in English.

English and Russian have different grammatical ways of using collective pronouns. It is common in Russian to use "we" in reference to two people where English would use "I." For example, "Katya and I went to the store," in Russian would be "We with Katya went to the store." It is possible then that native Russian speakers would use "we" more frequently as grammatical transfer when speaking English. In the analyses below, I have tried to include examples from native speakers of both languages to demonstrate that the phenomena I am pointing to are not solely determined by the grammar of the first language of the parent.

Following Schiffrin (2002), the interviews were analyzed quantitatively and qualitatively for the occurrence of referring terms "we" and "they" and the topical entity (i.e., children, parents, whole family, or others) of the pronouns. Results from the single parents in the data set were compared to those from partnered parents to examine differences in referring to children and parents or the family unit as a whole. In order to compare the use of the singular first-person vs. the plural first-person pronouns in the single parent and partnered parent interviews, I compiled the interview data from these two groups of participants and coded the pronouns "we," "they," "us," and "you" using the find function in Word. The number of pronouns was calculated in relation to the number of words in the whole interview transcript. The use of "we" was then coded for referent—either as parent + child or parent + adult as interpreted in the local discourse (examples below).

We+Us in Parent Interviews

The amount of data from each group was similar, with 31,149 words produced in the single parent interviews and 31,109 in the partnered interviews (Table 2.2). The frequency of use of a collective first-person pronoun ("we" or "us"), however, varied across the two groups. Partnered parents used "we" or "us" almost twice as many times (490) as the single parents (252). However, it turned out in closer examination of the data that this difference in the use of "we" and "us" could be attributed to one participant.

Table 2.2 'We' and 'Us' in Interviews

	Total words	Total we+us	We+us/total words
Single parents (N=5)	31,149	252	.008
Partnered parents (N=5)	31,109	490	.015

Table 2.3 'We' and 'Us' in Interviews with Kevin Excluded

	Total words	Total we + us	we+us/total words
Single parents (N=5)	31,149	252	.008
Partnered parents (N=4)	31,109	285	**.009**

Kevin, the father in Family 2 above, used "we" and "us" frequently in the interview—a total of 205 times in 36 minutes of talk. When his contribution to the data was subtracted, the frequency of use of "we" and "us" in the interviews was only slightly higher than that of single parents (Table 2.3).

In this case, about .8 percent of all words in the interview were a collective first-person pronoun for single parents (N=5), and about .9 percent for partnered parents (N=4). Native Russian speakers in these data did not show a higher frequency of the use of the collective first-person pronoun. While the topic entity or referent for the use of "we" or "us" by a partnered parent seems straightforward, that is, referring to the speaker and their partner/spouse, the topic entity for single parent use of "we" and "us" was ambiguous, as I will discuss below.

The Topic Entity of "We" and "Us"

While single and partnered parents did not vary much in the frequency of use of "we" and "us" in the interviews overall, they did vary in the way that they used these pronouns. More specifically, the referent or topic entity to which the "we" or "us" referred was different for the different sets of parents. When the data were coded for the closest interpretable referent of "we" or "us," it was found that single parents were more likely to use "we" to include children than partnered parents were (Table 2.4):

Table 2.4 Interpretable Referents of "we/us" as Percent of Total Mentions by Parents

	Parent + child(ren) (%)	Parent + other parent or adult (%)
Single parents	65	35
Partnered parents	23	77

In some cases parents used "we" to refer to themselves and another adult such as a teacher, babysitter, or sibling who helped with the adoption. But in many cases, the use of "we" by single parents was ambiguous or was a direct reference to the parent and one or more children. There was almost an inverse relationship between single parents' and partnered parents' use of "we" and "us" with single parents including children in the collective pronoun 65 percent of the time, and partnered parents including only their partner or spouse 77 percent of the time. Such discursive differences in the interviews point to the ways in which children are constructed as active decision makers and joint collaborators in single parent talk about family language and education as children interactionally and discursively took the place of other adults in the conversation.

Partnered Parents' Use of "We"

Pronominal use can be ambiguous, but some of the clearest examples of the use of "we" and "they" in the data set came from married parents who contrasted the adult family members (parents) as "we" and the children as "they" in the interview talk. In the following excerpt, adoptive parent Kevin (a married father) is comparing the language development of his adopted children "our kids" to other children they met in the community "they."

> **Excerpt 2.4 "They had bestest"**
> (Study 1)
> Kevin: **They** [other children] had things like "bestest" and stuff like this, six-year-old speak, and **we** were like, my god, you know **our** kids don't use this because **they're** in a controlled environment you know and **their** language is good.

While the two different groups of children (other people's children and "our kids") are both "they" in the excerpt, "we" refers to Kevin and his wife who are observing or reflecting on their children in the narrative.

Kevin's use of "we" was high as noted above, but he was not the only partnered parent to refer to the children as "they" and parents as "we." A similar process occurs in the following excerpt from adoptive mother Kathy who refers to her daughter as "she," and the adults as "we."

Excerpt 2.5 "We don't know where she's going to level off"
(Study 2)
> Kathy: And just start tackling it [learning the alphabet] a little bit at a time. It's not coming really, really fast. I mean **she** is picking it up, and there maybe some delays that she never overcomes. I mean **she** had fetal alcohol syndrome, **her** mother was an alcoholic, so **we** just don't where **she's** going to level off. You know, so…

Here the use of "we" is ambiguous (is it Kathy and her husband, the parents and teachers, other advisors or professionals?), but "we" does not seem to include the daughter here as the daughter is referred to as "she" and is constructed as the observed child tackling challenges with the adults watching to see "where she's going to level off." By constructing the daughter as the observed and herself with other adults as the observers, there is not a sense of a collaborative, "we're in this together" attitude between mother and daughter (as we will see below with single father John). In addition, the aspects of the child's history mentioned in the utterance (fetal alcohol syndrome and parental alcoholism) were most likely not regularly discussed with the seven-year-old daughter, making a collective "we" that included the daughter as collaborator less likely.

Single Parents

Single parents had more ambiguous uses of "we" where there was no other adult partner who could be included in the collective meaning of "we" with the adult speaker, and thus the default understanding was that "we" referred to the parent and the children. This "we" that refers to the parent and child(ren) occurs in John's interview below:

Excerpt 2.6 "We're still doing that kind of tracking"
(Study 2)
> Lyn: So he didn't have any literacy skills in Russian?
> John: No. So right now **he's** learning to write, **he's** learning to write in English. It's the first time **he's** learning to read and write. **He's** still trying to figure out the, you know, **you** read from left to right and there's a word on the page for the word **you** speak. **We're** still doing that kind of tracking.

Like Kathy's quotation in Excerpt 2.5 above, the question I ask, "So he didn't have any literacy skills in Russian?" and John's response place the child (Sasha) in the observed ("he") position, with the adults constructed as observers of his literacy development. However, unlike Kathy, John shifts the pronominal use and perspective of the discourse by including himself as a participant in Sasha's learning to read as he moves from "he" to "we" in the statement: "We're still doing that kind of tracking." Like in Kathy's quote, the "we" here is ambiguous—does we refer to John and Sasha or John and another adult? The verb "tracking" and the preceding discourse, however, point to the first interpretation as the tracking refers to the process of decoding the direction of text and identification of words on the page. John doesn't contrast the "we" to "he" in the utterance as Kathy does above "we don't know where she's going to level off," and as was discussed above in the question analysis, John was a highly collaborative interlocutor with his children. Rather than an evaluative statement about the child's abilities, John talks about the kind of work it takes to learn how to read and makes this a joint effort (with the child and possibly other adults).

A similar ambiguous use of "we" occurs in single mother Lucy's interview where she talks about reading Russian language books with her daughter.

Excerpt 2.7 "We read from those books every night"
(Study 2)

> Lucy: **We** have bought Russian children's stories [//] two books of Russian children's stories when I was in Russia and brought those home with me to read. **We** read from those books every night [//] just about every night maybe just a couple times.

While the first "we" in "we have bought …" could refer to Lucy and her sister (who traveled with her to Russia) or other adult, the only clear referent in the discourse for "we" in "we read from those books every night" is Lucy and her daughter. It is also important to note here that Lucy was a single mother and one of the few adoptive parents who reported reading in Russian to their child, further suggesting that single adoptive parents might accommodate to children through learning and using their heritage languages as single father John had also done. After conducting these types of interviews for several years and being puzzled by these kinds of ambiguous "we's," in the more recent project of Russian-speaking mothers (conducted during 2016–17), I finally stopped an interview and asked a mother what she meant by "we":

Excerpt 2.8 "We're still happy"
(Study 3)
Elena: We really liked [the school], we're still happy, she's still there in the fourth grade, happy with it.
Lyn: I'm sorry, when you say "we" do you mean your daughter and yourself? hhh?
A: yeah, yeah, **it's we**, because we go everywhere together...

The mother in this excerpt is a native speaker of Russian (see also Chapter 3), and Russian uses a collective "we" in the subject position more frequently than English. However, the example above is not a case where this "we" would necessarily occur. When asked about her use of "we," Elena states that she does in fact mean her daughter and herself. In later conversation, she talked about letting her daughter make decisions about the activities she participated in and that specifically the daughter had chosen to go to theater classes on the weekends. While certainly these processes also occur in partnered and married parent families, single parents talked about family events and decisions differently and were more likely to include children in the collective subject position.

Single Parents Are Different

The differences in the use of first-person plural pronouns in single vs. partnered parents' interviews are important because they suggest differences in which children are made more active decision makers and collaborative partners to single parents in these families. In the single parent interviews (John, Lucy, and Elena), children are constructed as collectively engaging in their own learning processes, being satisfied with their parent's decisions, and making decisions with the parents themselves. Schiffrin (2002) has argued that pronominal use as a discursive resource is used to show in-group membership, belonging, and identity. Here, the parents being interviewed focus on a particular constellation of family members who are relevant to the topics in the interview questions. Here, partnered parents (Kevin, Kathy) referenced the other parent as a primary decision maker, while single parents were more likely to talk about these processes as collaborative, co-constructed events in the family sphere.

Both English-speaking and Russian-speaking parents showed this pattern, indicating that this is not a language-related effect even though Russian speakers commonly use the plural first-person pronoun to show actions where English speakers would use a singular first-person pronoun.

While De Houwer (2007) attributed the success of single parents in maintaining a minority language at home to an input-based explanation, from a construct-based approach, the success of single parents at bilingual parenting could be related to a variety of kinship processes demonstrated in this chapter. Single parents potentially construct and raise children as primary interlocutors, joint collaborators, and decision makers in the absence of other adults in the household. All of the families included in these interviews were parenting in a bi- or multilingual context, although not all of them spoke a language other than English with their families. There is no direct conclusion to be drawn about multilingualism and collective family identities in single parent homes from these data. However, in light of the findings of Obied (2010) and De Houwer (2007) discussed above, it may be that single parents feel more success in their family language policies or attempts to raise bi- and multilingual children not only because it is "natural" to use the minority or parent's first language, but rather because the parent has a different perspective to family life in which the child is a co-collaborator and a participant in decision making that includes using a minority language. At the very least, there is not a simple linguistic answer to this question, but rather an emerging discussion about language and its relationship to the parent-child relationship. In Chapter 3, I explore how minority language use, collaboration, and routine shape a mother-daughter relationship in Elena's family.

In the debate between family internal and family external processes, findings from single parent families suggest that family internal processes may play a greater role in mitigating external influences than often discussed. If single parents, through engagement and relationship building, are better at maintaining minority languages (a hypothesis that requires more rigorous, focused study), then the internal bond, belonging, and identity all play a role in children's multilingual experiences.

3

Walking to School in Russian: Constructing a Mother-Daughter Relationship

Single mother-headed families make up a significant number of households across the United States and globally. According to the 2011 US census, there are about 13.7 million single parents in the United States and about 24 percent of all children (75 million) under the age of eighteen live in a single mother family. Most single parents in the United States are single as a result of divorce, and, despite common stereotypes, single mothers in the United States are older in age than married mothers and financially independent and stable. In 2011, The Organization for Economic and Cooperative Development (OECD) reported that worldwide, single parent households make up about 15 percent of all families with 85 percent of them headed by women. Despite the prevalence of single-mother families in the United States and worldwide, and the differences that single mothering must entail (e.g., greater disclosure of children's origins, joint construction of family identities, and involvement in social caregiving networks), there is very little family language research that focuses on single-mother families (cf. Navarro and Macalister, 2016; Obied, 2010; Poveda et al., 2014). This chapter focuses on an everyday routine, walking to school, that a single mother in the United States described as an important time when she and her daughter could use Russian. I examine here the walk to school as a rapport building activity where mother and daughter negotiate their relationship using Russian through talking about their past, present, and future lives.

As demonstrated in the previous chapter, a focus on single parents is important because interactional patterns within a family with only one adult present can be different from those in dual-parent families, and family construction processes are also different and potentially lead to greater involvement of children in family building and decision making (Poveda et al., 2014). While not all single parents ask as many questions as John in the previous chapter or are as conscious of their accommodation to their children, the interactional context of the single parent family is different than that of dual-parent families both qualitatively and quantitatively. In this chapter, I explore how the bilingual interactional patterns and routines of a single mother and an only-daughter construct their mother-daughter relationship and afford opportunities for kinship building.

More specifically, I focus on how the use of Russian intersects with the use of a strategy of "calling 'Mom,'" or using a kinship term as an attention getter and topic changer by the daughter at specific points during the walk to school. Through this analysis, I demonstrate how new topics, such as discussions about the mother's childhood, are introduced and connected to the daughter's current life experiences. These interactions construct a harmonious, bilingual mother-daughter relationship that is enacted in the walk-to-school routine. In contrast to the large number of studies focusing on children's resistance to parental language strategies and minority language use (my own included) (e.g., Fogle, 2012; Gafaranga, 2010; Said and Zhu Hua, 2017), this chapter provides evidence of engaged bilingual use on the part of the school-aged daughter.

Mother-Daughter Relationships

Obied (2010: 228) provided convincing evidence that single parent families have been left out of the research on bilingual parenting and argued that focusing on "the changing face of the bilingual family in the twenty-first century" can "highlight the challenges which these families face in their attitudes towards languages and cultures which inform their lives and relationships with each other." Obied concluded that single parents and non-residential parents are able to support bilingual children's biliteracy development, and that being divorced or single is not an obstacle in-and-of itself. However, in light of evidence that single parents might actually be better at maintaining a minority language in interaction with children as discussed in Chapter 2 (De Houwer, 2007), it seems reasonable to investigate more closely how these processes play out in interaction. More specifically, how does the use of the minority language intersect with the relationships in the family (as Obied [2010] seems to suggest above) and how do kinship relations or family roles emerge in the negotiation of bilingualism in the single parent family?

Mother-daughter relationships are known to be particularly fraught—as Tannen (2006: 11) writes:

> Many [adult] mothers and daughters are as close as any two people can be, but closeness always carries with it the need, indeed the desire, to consider how your actions will affect the other person, and this can make you feel that you are no longer in control of your own life.

This conflict between closeness and control plays out in interaction, as Tannen demonstrated in her book about mother-daughter talk, as mothers' advice and comments are often taken as criticism and instantiate the simultaneous but conflicting connection and control maneuvers that Tannen has identified in other discussions of family discourses (Tannen, 2007).

In single parent families, however, daughters in particular have been found to thrive. Coontz (2016) notes that while divorce can affect children both positively and negatively, in some divorced, female-headed families, daughters were caring, competent, self-confident, popular, and high achieving. These girls often assumed caretaking responsibilities (for younger siblings or older family members) alongside their mothers, and the family structure had a positive effect on their well-being (Coontz, p. 103). Coontz goes on to cite Mavis Hetherington that some children of divorced parents "emerge as psychologically enhanced and exceptionally competent and fulfilled individuals." In the bilingual mother-daughter relationship discussed in this chapter, we see how mother-daughter interaction, routine, and the use of Russian connect the family to past and future as they construct a family identity during walk-to-school conversations.

Walk to School

Language socialization research focused on daily routines as a way to locate the socialization of novices or children into linguistic and cultural norms

(Ochs, 1988; Ochs and Schieffelin, 1984). Interactional routines such as call and response in non-Western cultures were found to facilitate language development in ways not previously discussed in the language acquisition literature. In addition, family routines in Western contexts such as mealtimes (Blum-Kulka, 1997; Ochs and Schieffelin, 1984) and book reading and literacy events (Heath, 1982, 1983) emerged as important sites of language and literacy socialization. While there is a large body of sociolinguistic and family language research situated in mealtime conversation (cf. Blum-Kulka, 2008), many parents (and scholars) have noted that family mealtimes in two-working-parent homes in Western contexts are declining (Ochs and Kremer-Sedlik, 2013). Other contexts or activities, such as the ride to school or bedtime conversations, could be more important moments of parent-child interaction and socialization (Adler and Adler, 1984). For this reason, I have begun to ask families who participate in my studies to identify the most valuable times of family interaction for recording. For Elena, this was the walk to school that occurred every morning.

Walking methodologies are increasingly common in anthropological, education, and even linguistic landscape research (Lou, 2017; Nordstrom and Plascencia, 2017); however, there are very few studies of family language that involve family members moving through space. While my analysis in this chapter does not focus specifically on the language use in relation to movement and walking, there are moments in the recordings where events in the local context (a car passing or a squirrel in a tree) as well as passers-by affect the language use, in terms of content, function, and choice (i.e., Russian or English). Furthermore, in terms of timescales, a topic that has received much attention in sociolinguistics over the past two decades (cf. Blommaert et al., 2005; Lemke, 2000), the walk to school is a bound activity that has a specific duration and rhythm. Thus the walk to school as an activity constrains the amount and type of talk that can occur. In this time-bound context, important topics need to be introduced earlier rather than later, and speaking time, turn-taking, and other interactional aspects of the conversation must fit into the activity as I discuss below (cf. Scollon and Scollon, 2003). Considering the constraints placed on family conversations by the activity in which family members are engaged further augments the consideration of kinship processes, as the activity itself (of walking to school in this case) is a part of being kin or being mother or daughter. The repetition of the joint activity constitutes the family "doing" together and becomes a habitual event that characterizes the family and the mother-daughter dyad. In the sense that kinship is something that is done and is related to action (as discussed in Chapter 1), the walk to school and the talk that occurs during the walk to school, including Russian language use, is an important part of being and doing family for this mother and daughter.

The Family

Elena was a highly educated mother who had come to the United States as an exchange student and worked at a local university as a Russian professor. She had a ten-year-old daughter at the time of the study who attended a local, public elementary school. Elena, like John in Chapter 2, fit the single-parent-by-choice profile discussed in Poveda et al. (2014) as an educated and proactive older parent. In the initial interview I conducted with Elena, she stated that she saw being a single parent as normal and worked to normativize their family structure for her daughter:

Excerpt 3.1 "This particular arrangement is normal"
(October 2016)
> I don't know it's just (.) I consider it like any other family it's just to me either also it's normal and then what I'm telling my daughter that we have this ideal in mind but you know in reality that's not how it is and you know this particular arrangement is normal and that particular arrangement is normal.

In keeping with the single-mother parents in Poveda et al.'s study who reported involving their children in family decision making, Elena also saw her daughter as a companion and joint collaborator. As mentioned in Chapter 2, it was actually Elena's initial interview where I noticed a tendency to refer to herself and her daughter as "we" in relation to family decisions. Elena noted that she and her daughter "went everywhere together," and her daughter made her own choices about the activities in which she participated (theater, for example). In general, there was not much outward conflict between mother and daughter in the walk-to-school recordings, although, in a few cases, Maria indirectly made suggestions about future plans that seemed contrary to her mother's original ideas and in one case noted that she had not been listening to her mother's talk (after a longish monologue on a difficult topic).

Another aspect of Elena and Maria's relationship that stood out for me in relation to other parents with bilingual children I had interviewed in the United States was Elena's satisfaction with both Maria's Russian language competence and her own family language policy. She felt that Maria spoke Russian well and attributed this primarily to the annual trips to Russia that she and her daughter made in the summers. In the following excerpt, I asked her if her family in Russia supported her in raising a bilingual child:

Excerpt 3.2 "Maria is practically indistinguishable"
(October 2016)

    A: and you know my family seems to uh, salute my choices and support my choices and—and you know seem to be very proud of the fact that Maria comes to Russia and is practically indistinguishable
    L: yeah!
    A: from other kids.

In the data below, we see that Elena accepts Maria's utterances no matter what language she uses though she herself uses Russian in most cases (cf. Gafaranga, 2010). Unlike the conclusions drawn in other studies of family language policy in which the child's use of the majority language is interpreted as resistance and an internal shift toward English or dominant language, here Elena most often maintains Russian and does not herself switch. Rather it seems that she accepts an ebb and flow in her daughter's competence and knows that she will be more productive in Russian after the summer trip home. The family bilingualism follows a yearly cycle of dominance where Russian is dominant in the summer, and English more prevalent in the spring. However, there are many examples in the data when Maria does choose (whether conscious or unconscious) to initiate conversation in Russian with her mother (see Excerpt 3.4 below). The level of acceptance of Maria's language production and competence on the part of Elena contributes to a harmonious relationship and perhaps mutual trust where Maria feels safe to try out Russian when she can.

The Data

When asked if she would follow up the initial interview with in-home recordings of herself and her daughter, Elena agreed noting that they usually spoke Russian on the walk to school and that would be the best time to do the recording. Elena lived in a high-rise apartment building near the elementary school that her daughter attended. She noted in the initial interview that the apartment and the ability to walk places reminded her of home in a Russian city.

Elena recorded twenty-nine walks to school over a period of about ten weeks. The average length of the walk to school over the twenty-nine recordings was 11 minutes. Altogether, Elena recorded about 5.5 hours of data (Table 3.1). I walked with Elena and her daughter to school on the last day of recording to videotape the route so that I would have a sense of the physical structures and possible obstacles that intersected with the talk on the audio recordings. Not all of the data were transcribed because the sound quality was poor (the recorder was sometimes in Elena's bag or the sounds of traffic made it hard to hear the speakers). All of the recordings were reviewed aurally, and the time of all uses of "mom" as an attention getter was noted in an excel sheet (as well as a note about the resultant discourse—if it was a new topic, complaint, narrative, suggestion, etc., as discussed in more detail below). I chose to code uses of "mom" rather than the more obvious switches between English and Russian in the conversations because I wanted to foreground the relationship between the mother and daughter and explore the language use from a kinship perspective. Family members talk about being family perhaps more than an outsider would expect, but I did not think that I would find explicit talk about kinship in every recording. Calling "mom" was a strategy that I noticed Maria used frequently, it indexed the parental relationship and mother-daughter relationship (if subconsciously), and it turned out to function in interesting ways in the discourse (including to change the language interaction from Russian to English). From the examples of "mom," excerpts that were theoretically relevant to the current discussion about bilingual language use, mother-daughter relationship, and the use of kinship terms were transcribed for this chapter.

Table 3.1 Walk-to-School Recordings

Recording	File name	Date of upload	Length
1	160108_0004	February 24, 2017	10:55
2	160109_0005		10:33
3	160111_0006		09:19
4	160112_0007		15:00
5	160120_0008		No data
6	160121_0009		10:34
7	160121_0010		16:14
8	160124_0011		No data
9	160126_0012		15:15
10	160127_0013		08:53
11	160203_0014		15:28
12	160204_0015		05:48
13	160205_0016		14:33
14	160209_0017	April 13, 2017	16:22
15	160212_0018		15:14
16	160217_0019		15:36
17	160218_0020		09:56
18	160301_0021		11:22
19	160303_0022		11:38
20	160310_0023		11:35
21	160316_0024		10:15
22	160322_0025		13:14
23	160324_0026		08:35
24	160329_0027	May 3, 2017	11:59
25	160401_0028		10:54
26	160405_0029		11:45
27	160407_0030		10:14
28	160407_0031		00:02
29	160413_0032		11:02

In general in the recordings, the walk to school was a relatively peaceful event. Elena and Maria did not seem to be in a rush to get out of the door, and they did not worry about being late, encountering traffic, or other issues associated with driving to work and school (although at times Maria did ask what time it was during the walk, though this might have been because they were early). The walk afforded time for talk as neither mother nor daughter wore headphones, and there was no radio playing. There were, at times, phenomena in the local surroundings that gave them something to talk about (a bird in a tree, a passer-by, etc.). The pace and timing of the walk also seemed to play a role in the conversation that ensued.

The walk to school was an event where Elena and Maria spent a lot of time doing rapport building and identity work. Much of the talk on these walks involved Maria describing her school life to her mother, talking about her social life, friends, and culture, and talking about language. A list of topics that I noted in the conversations can be found in Table 3.2.

Table 3.2 Topics of Conversation on the Walk to School

Planning for day ahead
Talk about controversial/difficult topics
Discussion of politics/elections
Talk about race and ethnicity
Talk about future
Considering hypothetical situations
Discussion of school topics (books, sports, etc.)
Talk about family—we walk to school, we do x
Metalinguistic talk (English and Russian)
Singing
Talk about pop culture
Retelling conversations with friends
Complaints (about the recorder, household tasks, etc.)
Talk about the weather
Greeting friends/neighbors/passers-by

In addition, walking to school for Elena and Maria was an activity that was part of their family identity. In at least one instance, Maria commented on the fact that they were unlike other families because they walked to school on a daily basis as she stated, "we walk every single day."

Excerpt 3.3 "We walk every single day"
(Recording 9, minute 7:03)
(Russian language is transcribed in Cyrillic, transliteration on the next line, then translation on the third line)

1	Maria:	I'm kind of mad at like (.) kind of the lazy people,
2	Elena:	да
		da
		yes
3	M:	xxx
4	E:	xxx
5		yeah who just like walk (.) one block
6	M:	mhm
7		cause we walk EVERY single day.
8		I don't think there's a day when we DON'T walk.
9	E:	xxx
10		xxx не умеюм
		xxx ne umeyum
		xxx *we can't*
11		конечно можем ходить.
		konechno mozhem hodit.
		of course we can walk.
12	M:	xxx
13		remember when Andrey was complaining,
14	E:	mhm
15	M:	About walking so much?
16	E:	мхм а - в Нью Йорке, да?
		mhm ah - v New Yorke, da?
17	M:	yeah
18	E:	Uh-hu:h,
19	M:	xxx

20	Cause we:,
21	like (.) we WALK all the time,
22	We don't even have a CAR
23	so we don't get to choose to walk

In this excerpt, Maria compares herself and her mother to the "lazy people" who don't walk much. Walking in this short excerpt is constructed as an everyday, routine practice that sets Maria and Elena apart from other Americans in Maria's eyes. Maria notes that she and her mother walk every day and that "we don't get to choose to walk." While Maria compares herself and her mother to "lazy people" and "Andrey who was complaining," suggesting that she and her mother are stronger and more energetic than other Americans, Elena orients to this episode as a complaint from her daughter. She begins to explain that they could take the bus on some occasions. Maria's final statement, "we don't even have a car so we don't get to choose to walk," does seem to evaluate her mother's decisions negatively or at least to note that she (Maria) does not have control over this situation despite the fact that she has constructed the act of walking as a positive aspect of their everyday life. In short, Maria constructs walking as a part of her everyday routine with her mother and something that sets herself and her mother as a family apart from other Americans and/or friends. Maria doesn't talk about the relationship of walking to their Russian heritage (she rather relates it to the cost of owning a car and paying for gas in the continuation of the conversation). Elena most likely walked most places as a child and young adult in Russia (the number of car owners has nearly doubled in Russia between 2005 and 2015 and was at only 36 percent of the Russian population in 2006 [Poushter, 2015; Radio Free Europe, 2012]). Walking then is also tied to Elena's Russian identity and set of practices that would have been a part of her own socialization growing up and owning a car possibly seen as a luxury or at least unnecessary expense.

Kinship, Routine, and Bilingual Talk

As established above, the walk to school was a routine activity that allowed time and space for Elena and Maria to build rapport, talk about Maria's social world and events at school, explore Elena's past experiences and opinions, and plan for the future. This was a time when Maria and Elena got to do being daughter and mother as they worked out both small and big questions (and sometimes small questions led to bigger ones) and formed roles, relationships, and identities. One particularly salient practice during the walk time (at least to a researcher interested in kinship) was the use of the kinship term "mom" or "mama" by Maria to interrupt her mother or get her mother's attention and introduce a new topic. The use of kinship terms in interaction has not been very well studied in linguistics (cf. Sclafani, 2015), and I discuss this gap and the impact of studying the functions of kinship terms in discourse further in Chapter 6. In these data, calling "mom" was a way that Maria, the daughter, got the floor and took turns at talk and therefore was an interactional strategy that allowed her to achieve interactional agency (Al Zidjaly, 2009) in the conversation with her mother. For Maria, "mom" or "mama" functioned as an attention getter, changed the topic, introduced narrative, planning, and complaint discourse, and began difficult discussions about ethnicity and race. It also functioned as a discourse marker that could lead to code-switching or the introduction of a new language (English).

As a Russian teacher, Elena was very aware of her daughter's and her own use of Russian. They did not have a large community of Russian speakers around them (although there was a Russian teacher at Maria's school), and in the data I received there were not a lot of instances where the two languages are freely mixed or where a multilingual repertoire or translanguaging seemed to contribute to the whole meaning-making (cf. Li Wei, 2018). The use of Russian and English for this pair seemed to alternate across turns with one speaker initiating a topic in one language or the daughter "resorting to" English when she couldn't seem to find the words in Russian (something that Elena said happened more toward the end of the school year when the data for this study were collected). Although, in the data set itself, Maria tended to use more Russian in the later recordings perhaps because she was less aware of the recorder than she was in the beginning.

Connecting Past and Future

Interactionally, calling "mom" allowed Maria the agency to refocus the conversation on a topic of her choice. As mentioned above, these moments could be to introduce complaints, plans, or contradictions in response to her mother, but in some cases Maria brought up topics that seemed important to her own self-understanding and identity. In Excerpt 3.4, for example, Maria projected her identity into the future and asked her mother to comment on her physical appearance and its connection to her ethnicity (both of Maria's parents are Slavic). Here she involved her mother in a consideration about the "future Maria" and then the two collaboratively constructed who that person may be.

Excerpt 3.4 "When I grow up"
(Recording 4, minute 4:51)

1	Maria:	Mama!
2	Elena:	Hm?
3		M: Do you think I'm gonna look like a Russian girl?
4		or American girl?
5		or an American Russian girl
6	E:	Ah, xxxx
7	M:	When I grow up
8		When I grow up.
9		Like, xxx do you think I'll look like a Russian girl?
10	E:	Is there a difference between a Russian girl,
11	M:	Mhm!
12	E:	and an American girl?
13	M:	because American people usually have like their,
14		cause you can tell (.) if someone's a Russian xxx
15	E:	Ну (.) часто да, не всегда
		Nu (.) chasto da, ne vsegda
		Well, often yes, not always
16	M:	Yeah but like do you think I will (.) look more like a - a Russian girl?
17	E:	А это от тебя зависит
		A eto ot tebya zavisit
		Well that depends on you
18		как ты захочешь, так
		kak ty zahochesh, tak
		what you want to be, so
19	M:	no, I can't like change xxx
20	E:	well,
21		конечно есть славянские

22
    koneshno est' slavyanskiye
of course there's Slavic
мама славянка
mama slavyanka
mama is Slavic

Here Maria questions her own appearance, ethnicity, and identity and conveys the sense that her growing up or becoming is open-ended with multiple possibilities or outcomes. The pair disagree over how much looking American, Russian, or American Russian is a choice for Maria. Her mother responds that there really is no difference (Line 10, "Is there a difference between a Russian girl"). Maria responds, "you can tell" (Line 14). Elena seems to interpret "looking Russian" (or American) to have more to do with the changeable aspects of appearance (e.g., clothing, makeup, hairstyle, etc.), and this interpretation seems to make sense in the projection to the future as something that could evolve into being (and is not already present). Elena states that it is Maria's decision how she wants to look (Lines 17–18). But here Maria disagrees, saying that she can't change some things (evidently physical), and Elena agrees that she is Slavic (and her mother is Slavic) and, the intended meaning seems to be that some aspects of ethnicity are unchangeable.

The question that Maria asks in the beginning becomes irrelevant in her own line of argument—she first seems to suggest that there is a choice in looking American or Russian (perhaps by clothing or the way she carries herself as her mother seems to interpret the question) as the outcome is unknown, but then concludes that she looks Russian because of physical features that she can't change. Here Maria and her mother collaboratively work out Maria's fluid identities, with Elena attributing the choice to Maria, but Maria seeing herself as more Russian because of her physical appearance. Maria's question is aimed at understanding how people will see her rather than how she sees herself or will see herself, and this nuance could explain why she does not accept her mother's opinion that it is up to her. There is an underlying tension about what racial difference means, what it means to be Slavic in an Anglo American White society, and how others perceive these differences. More specifically, Maria seems to be negotiating the fact that there might be different kinds of "whiteness" or White ethnicities in the United States.

In the previous excerpt (Excerpt 3.3), Maria addressed her mother in English as was more common in the early recordings (that was the fourth one of the set). In a later recording (Excerpt 3.4), Maria addresses her mother in Russian to ask her about her own school experiences in Russia when she was Maria's age. Maria engages her mother in a discussion of her past schooling in order to understand her own present school system and to understand how things are done in her current school life. Here the differences between mother's and daughter's worlds become relevant. Maria introduces this topic with the attention getter "mama" and starts with Russian (though she switches to English in Line 8).

Excerpt 3.5 "When you went to school in Russia…"
(Recording 14, minute 7:47)

1	Maria:	Mama!
2	Elena:	[Mm?
3	M:	[Когда ты в школу ходила в России
		[Kogda ty v shkolu hodila v Rossii,
		[*When you went to school in Russia,*
4	E:	mhm,
5	M:	Ты в класcом занималас?
		Ty vklasom zanimalas?
		Were you in a class?
6	E:	ну
		nu,
		well,
7		как ска -
		kak ska -
		how to sa -,
8	M:	Like did you have different classes and stuff like that?
9	E:	Ты имеешь в виду support?
		Ty imeyesh' vvidu support?
		Do you mean support?
10		Было у нас как uh,
		Bylo u nas kak uh,
		We had uh,

11	M:	ни ни ни ни,
		ni ni ni ni,
		no no no no,
12	E:	А что?
		Ah, chto?
		Then what?
13	M:	But like where you could choose out classe:s,
14		like in middle school?
15		where if there was like a math class,
16		like you didn't have to go to all classes,
17	M:	Нет.
		Nyet.
		No.
18		У нас было по-другому
		U nas bylo po-drugomy,
		Ours was different,
19		У нас было расписание
		U nas bylo raspisaniye,
		We had a schedule,
20		когда з – занятие туда все должны ходить
		kogda z- zanyatiye, tuda vsye dolzhny hodit',
		where to go for the class, everyone was required to go there,
21	M:	There was a homeroom teacher,
22	E:	Da.
23	M:	And then,
24	E:	ну, классный руководитель
		nu, klassnyy rukovoditel',
		well, a lead teacher
25		и разные предметы
		i raznyye predmety
		And different subjects
26		нам нужно на них ходить всем
		nam nuzhno na nix hodit', vsyem
		we all had to go to them

27	но были некоторые занятия
	no byli nekotoriye zanyatiya,
	but there were some classes,
28	они назывались факультативы – факультативные занятия
	oni nazyvalis' fakultativy, fakul'tativnye zanyatiya
	they were called elective – elective courses
29	по желанию
	po zhelaniyu
	by choice
30	они уже были после уроков
	oni uzhe byli posle urokov,
	they were after the lessons,
31	после занятий
	posli zanyatiy
	after classes
32	Например, я ходила по – xxx на физику в девятом классе
	Na primer ya hodila po - xxx na fiziku, v devyatom klasse
	For example I went to – to Physics in the ninth grade
33	и ходила на факультатив по английскому
	i hodila na fakultativ po angliskomu
	and I went to the elective in English

Talking about past events in the language in which they occurred (e.g., talking about school topics in English and home topics in the home language) is a phenomenon noted by other multilingual family researchers (e.g., Cruz-Ferreira, 2006) and can help to explain why Maria chose to introduce this topic in Russian as it was related to her mother's Russian life experience. The use of Russian could also be attributed to the fact that the prior conversation had been ongoing in Russian.

In this excerpt, Maria is asking her mother if she had a choice in the classes she took in middle school, and when she is not able to convey this idea in Russian (Lines 7–8) she switches to English to explain what she means. Maria was currently in elementary school at the time of the recording, but in this episode she seems to be thinking about or planning for middle school as she explains to her mother in Line 14. Here Maria is asking about her mother's past in order to make sense of her own future and, possibly, to find out if her mother is prepared to advise her on the possibilities for middle school in the United States. Thus asking about her mother's past in Russian is related to Maria making sense of her own experience in the future in the US school. As was seen in Chapter 2, the person who asks the questions transfers the conversational burden to the other interlocutor. Here Maria is questioning her mother and while there is some confusion and negotiation over the question itself (Lines 5–10), Elena takes the floor and continues an explanation in Russian for several lines. Elena is very consistent with her Russian language use, but she is accepting of either language from Maria.

This episode continues in the following excerpt (Excerpt 3.6), as Maria interrupts her mother's talk in Russian to reintroduce the topic of middle school a second time "Mama? In middle school … " and here switches to Russian to indicate where "v Amerike," (in America) (Line 3) do you get to choose out your classes. This question is almost exactly the same question that Maria asked her mother about her own experience in Russia in Excerpt 3.5 above except now she has switched contexts to the United States and asks her mother what she knows about middle school here.

Excerpt 3.6 "To prepare for middle school"
(Recording 14, minute 8:58)

1	Maria:	Mama?
2		In middle school,
3		в Америке,
		v Amerike,
		in America,
4	Elena:	Uh-huh,
5	M:	Do you get to choose out your classes?
6		or, no.
7		Cause I read this book
8	E:	некоторые -
		Nekotoriye –
		Some -
9		Некоторые да
		nekotoryye, da
		some, yes

10	M:	xxx some classes,
11	E:	хххх, да.
		xxxx, da.
		xxxx, da.
12	M:	Classes you go to, so like Math,
13		and
14	E:	да.
15	M:	English
16	E:	да. English,
		Da. English,
		Yes. English,
17	M:	You know what I think - I think fourth and fifth grade,
18	E:	Mhm,
19	M:	Uh, it's a xxx to prepare for middle school,
20	E:	Uh-huh,
21	M:	And, uh,
22		It saves the (.) school money.
23	E:	Mhm.

At the end of this episode, Maria begins to guess why schools in America switch classes, "it saves the school money" (Line 20). She also notes that she learned about switching classes from a book she read, and seems to be educating her mother about the school system and the experiences she will have that her mother did not. Here Maria's questions do not lead to longer turns from her mother, but rather give her an opportunity to talk about what she herself knows about the US school system. Bilingual second-generation children often play the role of expert about the new school system and language broker in relation to their parents, and practices such as translating for parents at school can be beneficial in recognizing school children's bilingual competencies (Cline et al., 2010). Maria's mom Elena is a professor at a US university and highly proficient in English, so the types of language brokering described in the research literature were not necessary for Maria, but in these two examples, Maria is testing out her mother's knowledge about middle school in the United States and determining the major differences between the United States and Russia. Maria approaches this topic with some caution as she asks her mother first about her own experience rather than immediately pointing out that middle school will be different for her in the United States.

In these two episodes, Maria considers how her experience is different and will be different from her mother's own school experiences. She does not respond to her mother's answers about her schooling in Russia, but introduces a related topic (in English) in Excerpt 3.6 that she had read in a book that she would be able to choose classes in middle school (and asks her mother if this is true). Here the differences across generations and national settings allow mother and daughter to build shared knowledge about schools and schooling and for Maria to learn about her mother's past and to project that past into the future. Ochs (1994) made the point that some conversational narratives, specifically stories, can "step into the future" and by telling about past events, predictions can be made about the future. While the excerpts above are more explanatory than narrative by Labov and Waletzky's (1967) definition of narrative, that is, there is very little temporal sequencing, Maria's elicitation of Elena's memories about her past allows for Maria to make predictions about her own future through comparing her mother's past in Russia to what she knows and what she has read in the United States. Maria starts to use Russian in Excerpt 3.6 (and Excerpt 3.5), but finding the topic hard to explain in Russian (perhaps because her own school experiences had not been in Russian), she switches to English for explanations and follow-up questions. Thus while talking about Elena's past in Russia is an opportunity to use Russian, hammering out the details of US schooling is done in English.

Russian Teachers and Walks to School

The walk to school provided Elena and Maria an interaction-rich time in which they could manage their schedules and responsibilities as well as work on larger identity work projects, such as learning and maintaining Russian and understanding the differences between Russia and the United States as well as their own experiences in the past and projected experiences in the future. Maria introduced new topics into the conversation during the walk by using the attention getter and kinship term "mom." "Mom" invoked the mother-daughter relationship in the conversation and opened the floor for Elena's opinion and advice on the topics related to Maria's identity as a Russian American girl and a comparison of her future experiences in middle school with her mother's past schooling. As in other studies of multilingual parenting, in these two excerpts, Maria uses Russian to talk about topics related to the family's Russian language experiences and lives and English to talk about her (English language) school life. Despite the parallel conversation in English and Russian documented in these walks, Elena reported being very happy with her daughter's Russian language competence. In addition to summer trips home to visit family, routine activities such as the walk to school where Elena could count on an uninterrupted time to use Russian provided opportunities not only for language learning and use but also for mother-daughter bonding and understanding.

The casual way in which Elena and Maria built rapport in a bilingual medium and Elena's acceptance of Maria's English language use as well as her attempts to use Russian demonstrates how the mother-daughter relationship, routine activity, and types and medium of talk came together in this family. Furthermore, the use of "mom, mommy, mama" tags and talk about their family identity allowed for a forging of an interactional space within the routine activity where family could be done and explored and the daughter had an opportunity to negotiate the conversation.

Being a Russian Teacher

Despite being a single parent, which is often constructed in research as a position of deficit or disadvantage as discussed above, Elena and her daughter occupied a privileged position as a White, educated, and highly literate family. Elena held a prestigious university job and was a trained Russian language teacher. Despite the growing number of studies on family language policy and outcomes in bilingual parenting, we know very little about what effect being a language teacher has on raising (one's own) bilingual children. Teachers and researchers have certainly documented their own children's multilingual development (e.g., Caldas and Caldas-Caron, 2002; Cruz-Ferreira, 2006), and these reports seem rather positive. However, in the small amount of data I have with Russian-speaking mothers in the South, I have not found that being a Russian teacher necessarily facilitates raising a Russian-speaking child.

At least two other mothers I interviewed for the Russian-speaking mothers project (in which Elena initially participated) taught Russian in school or university. Both of these mothers were married to English-speaking, American men and both reported not using Russian with their children. In addition, I have known a few Russian teachers through my own networks in the South and anecdotally know that these mothers also did not try to use Russian at home. In contrast, the two single mothers in the data set, however, reported that they were able to maintain Russian with their children. In a context where there is not an identifiable Russian-speaking community, such as in the smaller cities of the US South, mothers in mixed marriages may find it easier to assimilate to US culture and language and save their Russian for the classroom if they are language teachers.

Conclusions

Including single parent families in research on multilingual families then has clear theoretical implications for research on multilingual language use and maintenance. In Chapter 2, I demonstrated that single parents potentially interact with their children differently than partnered parents because of the adult-child ratio and structural differences that lead to different patterns of accommodation and potentially different expectations for interaction. In addition, in keeping with prior studies that had found single parents to include children in collaborative decision making more frequently, I found that single parents talk about their children differently in interviews and tend to use a collective "we" subject to create a collective family identity. In the current chapter, I have further investigated a single mother-daughter relationship that demonstrates how these processes play out in a daily activity (the walk to school). While walking to school only took 11 minutes, repeated over time, this activity provided a space for the pair to use Russian regularly and talk about past and future lives in a collaborative manner that allowed the daughter opportunities to construct her identities, explore cultural and social differences with her mother, and experiment with language without distractions from other family members, digital media, or competing demands.

To return the initial question of Chapter 2, which has guided these discussions, De Houwer found that single parents reported using more minority language than married parents in her 2007 study. The data presented in this chapter bear this out—Elena continued to use Russian even when her daughter switched to English. Therefore, while Maria's production was not always in Russian, the input in the conversation was. This tenacity on the part of the single mother could account for her overall satisfaction with the family language policy and Maria's ability to use Russian in the summer trips to Russia.

Walking to school, along with the use of Russian and Russian American identities, set this family apart from other families as Maria noted in Excerpt 3.4. Walking itself could promote interaction and learning as neuroscientist Shane O'Mara (2019: 13) notes: humans are "cognitively mobile," and that "walking markedly changes activity in the brain in subtle, important and powerful ways" (p. 17). While there is no evidence (yet) to suggest that walking promotes bilingual acquisition or even bilingual language use, the routine activity of walking to school provided time and space for Elena and Maria to talk about life and use Russian. This practice emerged as an identity marker that set them apart from other US families and intersected with the potential benefits (pacing, interaction, movement, engagement with the environment) that walking itself might have brought to these processes.

Finally, much research on single parents (reviewed in Chapter 2) has pointed to the ways in which children in single parent families achieve greater agency and involvement in joint decision making. While I chose to focus on episodes in this chapter that were related to connecting Elena's past life in Russia with Maria's present life in the United States, Maria herself directed much of these conversations. She asked the questions and opened the topics that were relevant to her understanding of herself and her schooling. She also found ways to negotiate her mother's knowledge and contribute to the construction of her projected future by answering her own questions (as in Excerpt 3.6). The mother-daughter relationship was built through these discussions and routine activities. Both Elena and Maria were busy with career, school, and after-school activities, but the 11 minutes a day provided an interaction-rich time to explore language, relationships, and identities for this family.

4

Adoptive Families: Constructing Competence, History, and Knowledge

The study of transnational, transracial, and queer adoption has arguably been one of the most influential forces in renewing an interest in kinship studies in the twenty-first century (cf. Homans, 2018; Volkman et al., 2005). Transnational adoption has also been a site of language socialization and identity research (Fogle, 2012; Higgins and Stoker, 2011; Lo and Kim, 2011; Shin, 2013). In the late 1990s to early 2000s, thousands of children were adopted from Eastern Europe by Western (US) parents. Powell and Montgomery (n.d.) report that in 2005, 46,000 children were adopted across borders, and that the United States was one of the largest receiving nations of children from abroad. These numbers have dropped as sending nations have halted international adoptions for various reasons. Russia stopped adoptions to the United States in 2012 in response to the US Magnitsky Act that placed sanctions on certain Russian officials. Thus international adoption is a political as well as a personal phenomenon, embedded in transnational power relations and individual kinships.

Fifteen years after the transnational adoption surge in the West, we know that children adopted transnationally navigate complex belongings that connect with their racial, ethnic, and linguistic identities (Higgins and Stoker, 2011; Yngvesson, 2010). In my own previous work, I have argued that the adoptive family is a negotiated family where children shape the interactional context of language use and learning (Fogle, 2012). In this chapter, I deepen the perspective on language in adoptive families to examine how transnational adoptive families negotiate family identity, kinship, and belonging through talk about the past and construction of prior competencies. In this chapter, I examine how adoptive parents and adopted children in my data interactionally negotiated these belongings and how children's past lives are linked to their current kinships and belonging in the adoptive family.

The data for this chapter were collected around 2005 and 2006 as I began work on two studies on language socialization and family language policy in Russia adoptive families (Fogle, 2012, 2013a). The first study, as discussed in Chapter 2, was an interview study with eleven adoptive parents who talked about language learning and educational decisions in their family. The second study (also introduced in Chapter 2) was a case study of three families whom I followed for eight months with school-age adoptees from Russia and Ukraine. In that study, I focused on how the children achieved interactional agency in family interactions and shaped the family discourse as well as their own language learning opportunities. In this chapter, I examine two interactional episodes, one from an interview with a mother Sarah (from the interview study) and the second from a conversation involving John (the father in Family 1 in Chapter 2) and his two sons (from the case study), that demonstrate how adoptive family members negotiated the complex processes of forming kinships and being family when family members have varying knowledge of and alignments toward each other's past histories, languages, and experiences.

Adoptive Parenting

Adoption researchers have consistently noted that adoption, typically understood as a contractual agreement that transfers kinship and caregiving responsibilities from a biological parent to other adults (either within kinship groups or between cultures and nations), both reproduces and transforms cultural norms (Esposito and Biafora, 2007; Homans, 2018). Depending on context, circumstance, and perspective, adoption can be seen alternatively as a positive solution for children or a harmful practice. As Homans notes:

> Adoption can adhere rigidly to nuclear family norms, regulating sexuality and contributing to the realization of racist projects, but it can also enable nonnormative family forms and it can queer the family. Adoption can mean the kidnapping of children from the Global South, even a form of slavery

meriting only abolition; but it can also reconceive family as part of larger, sometimes transnational, communities. Adoptees and adoptive families can be the same as everyone else; and they can be cyborgs, hybrids, uncanny assemblages (p. 2).

The small (but growing) body of work on adoption and family language has focused primarily on transnational adoption as a context of language contact, language learning, and bilingualism without much focused attention on critical approaches mentioned by Homans. Fogle (2012) for example argued that Russian and Ukrainian adoptees actively negotiated the interactional environment of the home and the strategies parents used to meet their language learning, bilingual, and identity needs. Shin's (2013) studies of Korea adoptive families showed how language learning played a role in culture keeping in these families and how learning Korean became a family project that involved parents and children leading to family bilingualism. While these accounts are generally positive, aimed at demonstrating how parents can accommodate to children's language backgrounds and language needs to establish belonging in the family, other studies focused on racial difference and the experiences of older adoptees have focused on the problematic issues of being transnational adoptees.

Studies of Korean adoptee returnees in particular have pointed out the complex negotiations of language, ethnic, and racial identities that are difficult for adult adoptees to navigate in their birth countries. Higgins and Stoker (2011) for example demonstrated the complex and difficult experiences of Korean returnees and how they constructed linguistic third space to counteract experiences of racism and rejection in Korean society. Lo and Kim (2011) further discuss the exclusion of a celebrity Korean adoptee and racialization, demonstrating that the perception of celebrity language competence in Korean was tied to kinship and regimes of citizenship. These studies have begun to build evidence regarding how language is an important part of adoptee belonging across the lifespan.

Critical adoption approaches can illuminate the study of language in the adoptive family (at the same time that linguistic studies can contribute to critical adoption research). The study of adoption can be realized as a way to improve the lives of children and the social institution itself, but from a critical perspective the study of adoption allows us to better understand society itself and "the structural inequalities—of race, of gender, of economic access, of geopolitics—that not only render contemporary adoption intrinsically unjust but that also characterize global social relations more generally" (Homans, p. 3). In this chapter, I attempt to apply a critical perspective more carefully to the adoption data I collected earlier in my career. Here I look at specific episodes in family conversation and interview data where parents talk to and about their children from a position of power (as White, English-speaking adoptive parents) and engage their children (in the first example) and me (in the second example) in understanding the children's own past experiences, histories, and learning. In doing this discursive work in these examples, the parents construct themselves as good parents by connecting with children's prior knowledge and competencies and bringing past kinships and experiences into the present time.

Risk

An important aspect of adoptive parenting that emerged in my earlier studies with East Europe adoptive parents was the fears that adoptive parents seemed to bring to the adoption process and parenting their adopted children. A pervasive discourse of risk, associated with adoptive parents' lack of knowledge about their children's ancestry, histories, and potentials, shaped family language policies and the maintenance of so-called birth languages in the interview and case studies I conducted. Adoptive parents reported fears about children's prior socialization in orphanages, possible fetal alcohol syndrome (see Excerpt 2.5 in Chapter 2), and exposure to abusive parenting or neglect (Fogle, 2013a). These fears influenced parents' beliefs about what languages should be used in communication with adoptees (with some parents fearing that sustained contact with Russian would remind the children of prior abuse or the orphanage context) and what kind of learners their children would be (i.e., that limitations to learning were possibly shaped by prior abuse). With no shared language between children and parents in most of these families, fears of risk in some cases became magnified because children might remain silent rather than using English or emerging bilingualism was inaccurately considered inadequate acquisition of Russian or English.

The fear of risk is also tied to privilege and power in relationships between adoptive parents and adoptees as well as sending and receiving nations. Adoptive parents in Western receiving nations with little experience with life in other countries and misunderstandings of cultures of care did not know how to judge or measure their children's past experiences and competencies. Lack of knowledge about normal second-language learning processes and bilingualism as well as a lack of competence in children's first languages (and inability to understand conversations during the adoption process) further led to misinformation where parents felt that their monolingual perspectives were correct and language differences seen as problematic or abnormal. Language delay and language disabilities (along with other psychological and cognitive disorders) were often attributed to adoptees because of a deficit view rather than examined in the context of normal trajectories or even the trauma associated with transnational adoption itself.

Some of the parents in my studies took steps to mitigate the power differentials between parents and adoptees, different cultural norms, and monolingual biases. However, all parents seemed to be confused by the competing explanations for children's bilingualism and learning and often expressed contradictory views. In this chapter, I revisit some of these data to better understand how parents made sense of their children's abilities and competencies as well as their past lives and identities. These data are important in showing that this kind of work emerged in narrative episodes within and about family and that understanding the silent experiences of children (that were lost in translation or through time) helped parents become more empathetic toward their children and see their children as experts with complex belongings across time and space.

Children's Experiences and Competence

Despite considerable discussion about the shortcomings of parental reports in documenting children's language, much of the research on bilingual parenting relies on parental reports of language use (by parents and children) collected through questionnaire and interview data. These studies take a relatively positivist view that what parents say family members do is what they do (despite findings to the contrary, cf. Coetzee 2018) and assume that the large numbers involved in the quantitative studies can mitigate any discrepancies. While these studies are helpful in understanding how parents view their language use and making possible correlations to bilingual outcomes, there is an attendant question that lingers—how do parents make estimations about their children's abilities and competencies? What background, stories, and routines influence parents' perceptions of their children's language production? We know for example that there is much variability in what parents perceive as a first word uttered by an infant, just as there must be variability in what is considered competent bilingual production. Bilingual competence is a social construct that varies across contexts and times (Fogle, 2013b; Lo and Kim, 2011). The data presented below represent interactional episodes where adoptive parents try to make sense of their children's pre-adoptive lives in contexts where the children cannot talk about their experiences (because of lack of a shared language) or children were not aware of the details of their past (e.g., what language their father spoke). In these episodes, the children's competencies and histories are constructed as increasingly complex by the parents as they negotiate the children's belongings and expertise. In terms of critical adoption research, these parents begin to negotiate the power differentials inherent in the transnational adoption phenomenon by acknowledging the children's histories and experiences as well as languages and their own parental ignorance. In relation to bilingual parenting and family language studies, the data show how parents' constructions of what children know (in first and second languages) emerge in narrative productions that connect children's competencies in context with their expertise and belongings.

In the analysis of two narrative episodes below, one family interaction in John's family (Chapter 2) and one narrative in an interview with an adoptive mother (other data from this interview study are presented in Chapter 2), I show how kinships, intimacies, and competencies are discursively constructed as parents observe their children and make hypotheses about their past lives. These processes are taken for granted in biological families where parents and children have not been separated and share histories. However, adoptive family processes are relevant to understanding how kinships are formed and how parents come to learn about their children. In addition, these examples start to normativize contexts where caregivers and children do not share language competencies, a phenomenon not uncommon in intergenerational multilingual families, and show how communication and kinship form without a shared language.

Many of the processes that lead to family formation in adoptive families are, I argue, linguistic. Not only can language be an important way of culture keeping for transnational adoptive families (Fogle, 2013a; Shin, 2014), the day-to-day negotiation and formation of family identities and relationships are done through language in interaction (Fogle, 2012). Parents of biological children take many things about their children for granted. They assume that their children will look like them, for one thing, which creates a sense of family belonging. They know that their children will share hereditary traits as well as, most likely, some personality and behavioral characteristics that create a sense of belonging. Even more than that, and perhaps something that both parents and researchers are less cognizant of, is the fact that some adoptive parents do not share in their child's early development and therefore do not know what their child knows. This lack of knowledge can be exacerbated by language differences where children are not able to answer questions or provide displays of their knowledge and competencies because they do not understand and are not understood by their parents. This lack of knowledge often leaves open a wide space for interpretation; and in the study of adoptive parents that I conducted, I found that parents relied on their own ethnotheories about child rearing and child development to explain their children's behavior (sometimes attributing actions to incomplete language acquisition, executive function disorder, and fetal alcohol syndrome). In the examples provided below, parents do not draw on these deficit views of their children but rather attempt to reconstruct children's past (pre-adoptive) lives in a way to provide more complex narrative about their histories when that knowledge had been lost. These discursive processes are tied to constructing belonging and legitimizing the adopted children's pasts as well as constructing the parents as good parents. The two examples below, in my opinion, show how important language is to forging children's identities and belonging as well as parents' understanding of their children's competencies. They further illustrate how adoptive families become family while acknowledging children's past belongings and socialization.

Narrative

Conversational narrative, or stories told in everyday interactions, according to Ochs and Capps (2001: 2), "imbue[s] life events with a temporal and logical order, to demystify them and establish coherence across past, present, and as yet unrealized experience." De Fina (2003: 369) further notes that narrative "both reflects social beliefs and relationships and contributes to negotiate and modify them." This chapter presents narratives in interaction from two different settings. In Poveda and colleagues' (2015) study of non-normative (single parent, gamete donation, and adoptive) family constructions, the authors point to narrative activities in the family as a central way in which families talk about children's origins and construct families. I use narrative analysis in this chapter in two primary ways: first, to show that being a parent is tied to understanding children's past lives, experiences, and histories; and second, to demonstrate how multilingualism plays a role in constructing the past kinships and competencies as well as the present family identities.

In this chapter, I examine a narrative from an adoptive mother in which she provides a very detailed account of how she learned that her children had competencies and skills she did not know about through observing their actions and how lack of a shared language made it hard to understand how much her children knew. I employ Labov and Waletzky's (1967) narrative structure to understand the structures of Sarah's more canonical, monologic narrative (cf. Ochs and Capps, 2001) to demonstrate how narratives are embedded within one another to create meaning. In John's data, which occur during a recording of family interaction, I focus more on the interaction between father and children and the possible kinships and identities that emerge through negotiation in the episode. In both episodes, narratives about the children's pasts intersect with the parents' construction of their own parenting relationships and roles as well as the linguistic and non-linguistic aspects of being a multilingual family.

The Transnational Adoptive Family Studies

The analysis of parents' constructions of their children's histories, kinships, and competencies below draws on two studies conducted in the Washington,

DC, metro area during 2007–8. The first study was an interview study with parents who had adopted Russian-speaking children at school age (aged seven or older) (Fogle, 2013a). This study was designed to understand the family language policies of Russia adoptive parents and how they made decisions about language and literature for school-age adoptees. While one of the primary goals of this study was to find out if adoptive parents were maintaining Russian, other topics included children's English language learning, literacy development, and adjustment to the school and family. The narrative selected for analysis below is from the interview data with one mother Sarah who had adopted a sibling group of four children from Russia.

Sarah's interview was conducted in her home and lasted about 52 minutes. It was the longest interview out of the eleven conducted for the study. One reason that Sarah's interview was longer than the others was because she told a slightly long story at the end of the interview in response to my closing question that generally asks, "Do you have anything to add or did I miss something?" This open-ended question gives the floor to the interviewee to discuss any topic that is on their mind or correct assumptions that might have emerged in the interview questions. Sometimes participants choose to discuss the goal of the interview or my investigation at this point or they will add something that suggests what they thought the goal of the study would be. The narrative provided by Sarah, however, seemed to counter a number of the questions I had asked about language in her family. As I discuss below, she provided her own take on what it's like to be a monolingual mom with bilingual children.

The second excerpt analyzed below is taken from the follow-up study (Fogle, 2012) to the interview study. This language socialization study followed three adoptive families (two of which had participated in the initial interview study) over a period of about eight months each. Parents in those families collected in-home recordings and family members took part in regular interviews. The excerpt below comes from the data of John's family. John was a single father who was a particularly proactive parent who valued interaction with his two sons who were adopted from Ukraine (as I discussed in Chapter 2). One thing that John did that other adoptive parents in my data did not do as much or as well was to encourage his children to remember, talk about, and make connections to their pre-adoptive lives in Ukraine. For a time, he kept in touch with the children's biological grandmother through telephone calls and, as in the excerpt below, he would engage the children in conversation about their past lives. Here I will focus more on the multiple kinships that are constructed through language and languaging as the family members talk about the children's past. So first, I will talk about Sarah's narrative about her children's competencies and then I will turn to John's family conversation about kinship and history.

Constructing Children's Knowledge and Competence

The rather lengthy (but important) narrative told by Sarah at the end of her interview was not prompted by any specific question, but rather produced in response to perhaps my orientation as a linguist toward the importance of language in her adoptive family throughout the whole interview. When asked if she had anything else to add, Sarah started to tell about the trip home from Ukraine and what her children knew had "nothing to do with their language" (as she states in Line 79). This long narrative sequence is made up of three embedded narratives in which Sarah tells about the trip from Ukraine to the United States when she brings the children home.

The first segment from Lines 1–19 tells about the first part of the plane trip and how the children were unsure about where they were and when they would land in America. This sequence served as a kind of narrative orientation to the second segment that began in Line 20 with an abstract (Labov and Waletzky, 1967), "But you know the resilience, which had nothing to do with their language necessarily," that opens a new narrative about the children getting lost in the Amsterdam airport and finding their own way back (despite not knowing English or their new names as Sarah notes). The third narrative introduced in the sequence begins in Line 53 where Sarah strengthens her claim that her children were aware of their surroundings and knew more than she thought they did (because of the language barrier). This third narrative begins with an abstract, "They have a lot more capability that you just don't see because of the language barrier," in Line 59. Altogether, the narrative sequence provides insight into how an adoptive mother learns about her children's knowledge and competence that were acquired before she met them and began her caretaking responsibilities and how her role as mother is shaped by these understandings. Sarah's sequence of narratives is also aimed at refuting the assumptions that I made in the interview that bilingualism and language learning were important for the children and the family. Sarah's illustrations of her children construct them as competent, resilient, and able to use previously acquired competencies in the new contexts without language. The three narratives here and the whole narrative sequence contribute to an understanding of the children's belonging in the new environment and the mother's construction of herself as a good mother. I have divided the long stretch of talk into three sections based on what I consider to be the start of new embedded narratives in order to provide analysis on each part.

Excerpt 4.1 'We had to go from Ukraine'
(February 2005)

1	Sarah:	You know because they are also like you know
2		cause we had to go from Ukraine
3		and then we went to Poland because that's where we had to process their visas.
4	L:	Uh-huh, yeah.
5	S:	And you know they were sort of explained, kind of, what the process was.
6		(By) you know the people there, and uhm
7		when we got to Poland they're like, 'Is this America?'
8	L:	Oh, ha-h-h-huh
9	S:	An- they didn't say, 'Is this America?' They said,
10		'America?' You know,
11		and we were like, 'No, not yet.
12		You know, we have to get on another plane and go for a much bigger [ride.'
13	L:	[mm-hmm
14		And we had a layover in Amsterdam.
15		(We) get off in Amsterdam,
16	L:	Mmm.
17	S:	'America?'
18	L:	Oh.
19		S: 'No.'

In this opening segment, Sarah situates the events in an orientation sequence "we had to go from Ukraine, and then we went to Poland." Here she describes the children as eager to land in America with repeated questions, "Is this America?" She also notes that the children had been told (presumably in their native language) what "the process was." However, in this first sequence, she constructs the confusion of the children in not knowing where they were and when they would land in America. This opening narrative sets the stage for the second narrative that is a more focused narrative of past events (Ochs and Capps, 2001) where Sarah tells a story about a specific event that has a climax and conclusion. While the children are constructed as confused and somewhat ignorant of what it was like to fly across continents in the above excerpt, in Excerpt 4.2 Sarah shifts this evaluation and talks about the children's "resilience" that has "nothing to do with their language" (Lines 20–1). The story she tells about losing the children in the airport corroborates this evaluation (Lines 23–44).

Excerpt 4.2 The resilience

20	S:	But you know th- uh-uh <creaky> the resilience,
21		which had nothing to do with their language necessarily
22		like we were in the airport in Amsterdam,
23		and Ksenia and Ma- uh Natasha needed to go to the bathroom,
24		so Mark had the other two, and I took them to the bathroom
25		and they're in the stalls, and then I decide I need to go,
26		So I'm like, 'O.k. I go.'
27		I come out.
28		They are nowhere to be found.
29		I am like frantic in the [airport. I'm
30	L:	⠀⠀⠀⠀⠀⠀⠀⠀⠀⠀⠀⠀⠀⠀⠀⠀⠀⠀⠀⠀[O:h.
31	S:	like, you know,
32		having them paged like over the system that these two little kids.
33		(And) they're like, 'What are their names?'
34		I'm like, 'They don't even know their names!'
35		[Like they know their first names, but they don't know [their last name you
36	I:	[O: h.⠀⠀⠀⠀⠀⠀⠀⠀⠀⠀⠀⠀⠀⠀⠀⠀⠀⠀⠀⠀⠀⠀⠀⠀⠀⠀[Yeah.

37	S:	know or whatever,
38		and they found their way back to him,
39		and it wasn't like just [down the hallway, it [was you know down the hallway,
40	I:	[Huh. [really?
41	S:	around the corner, make a turn
42	I:	uh-[huh
43	S:	[And I was like
44		beside myself.
45		I (was) like, I haven't even had these kids for like three days, and I've [lost them
46	I:	[<laughs>
47	S:	already! They're like Ahh!
48	S:	And uh, I was just really like thankful, I was like,
49		They are really aware of their [surroundings.
50	I:	[Oh, sure. [Yeah.
51	S:	[You know like
52	S:	this really.

In Excerpt 4.1, Sarah constructed herself as the expert who was guiding the children on the plane ride to the United States. In Excerpt 4.2, this characterization begins to shift. In the incident in the bathroom, the children become the experts by knowing how to get themselves back to their father when their mother was not present. In Lines 87–107, Sarah turns from telling the story of her children getting separated from her in the Amsterdam airport (they left the bathroom before she did) to commenting on her own role as a mother. Here she describes herself as "frantic" (Line 87) and constructs her decision to go into the bathroom stall herself a mistake because when she comes out the children are "nowhere to be found." She further builds her incompetence as a parent in telling about the conversation with airport officials and coming to the realization that the children "don't even know their names." In other words, as a parent she had not prepared the children for a situation in which they might be separated from her or need to know how to find her. And finally, in conclusion to the narrative (coda) she comments, "I haven't even had these kids for three days, and I've lost them."

Sarah portrays herself as a bad mother in this sequence because (a) she made a choice that led to her children being separated from her in the foreign airport, (b) she hadn't taught the children their names or identifiers, and (c) she lost the children within three days. In relation to the view of kinship as caregiving discussed in Chapter 1 (Flores, 2018), Sarah depicts herself as failing as a caregiver and draws on a model of the attentive, helicopter parent who shadows children's movement and autonomy and socializes children into fear of strange places and strangers (Ochs and Kremer-Sedlik, 2013; Tulviste and Ahtonen, 2007). The children, who had been socialized into caregiving models of independence where older children took care of younger children (Stryker, 2010), did not wait or look for their adoptive mother in the bathroom, but rather took matters into their own hands and found their way back to their father.

Sarah constructs herself as the confused and agitated adoptive mother who lost her kids in three days. She demonstrates how language was not a resource in this event and that paging the children over the loudspeaker with their names was not possible because the children did not know their names and likely would not pay attention to any announcements. Rather, the children relied on their own competence and self-sufficiency to solve the problem, and this resilience is tied to Sarah's understanding of their own self-reliance and growing trust in the children, "I was just really thankful … they are really aware of their surroundings." Getting to know her children's competencies without the help of language becomes a key point in the third and final narrative of the sequence. Here Sarah talks about her youngest child knowing how to do yard work without her teaching him how.

Excerpt 4.3 "Wow, I didn't know you could do that!"

53	S:	Cause you kind of, at least I did got the impression you know like
54		you know <clicks> you're talking to a two year old.
55	L:	Yeah.
56		Well, in some ways you are, and in some ways you're not.
57		They're not two.
58	I:	Uh-huh
59	S:	They have a lot more capability that because of the language barrier

60		you just don't see.
61	I:	Oh, uh-huh. Interesting.
62	S:	You know what I mean? So you're sort of treating them like they're totally
121		helpless
122	I:	Uh-huh.
123	S:	when in fact, they're not.
124	I:	Uh-huh.
125	S:	You know cause like even just stuff like uh
126		we went and helped my mom like
127		rake her leaves one day and
128		Andrew's gathering up all of the big sticks like out of the leaf piles,
129		and we're just kind of watching him,
130		and then he just starts to break them up into little pieces to put into the bag.
131		Like nobody's telling him to do this,
132		and he gets to a big piece that he can't break with his arms. So he puts it on the
133		ground, and he puts his leg on it, and then he snaps [it.
134	I:	[uh-huh
135	S:	You know, and we're like,
136		'O.k. how does a four-year-old know that?'
137		You know like clearly he's been taught that.
138		Not by us.
139	I:	Uh-huh.
140	S:	You know like he probably- that was probably you know
141		something they had to do at the orphanage
142		like help clean up the yard or you know whatever
143		and they teach them how to do you know different things. But I'm just like#
144		there's so much in their little heads that we have no idea
145	I:	mm-hm
146	S:	because of the language barrier
147	I:	uh-huh

| 148 | S: | you know that you're like, 'Wow, I didn't know you could do that.' |
| 149 | I: | <laugh> |

This story of doing yard work with her four-year-old son ends with a coda that encapsulates the theme of all three narratives together, "Wow, I didn't know you could do that," and summarizes the point of view of the adoptive parent who does not share knowledge of the children's worlds and histories and does not have access to the children's perspectives on their own lives because they do not have the language to share what they know and what they have experienced. In Lines 136 and 138, she notes that her son had been taught to pick up sticks and put them in the bag, but "not by us." "Us" here most likely refers to herself and her husband as the new caregivers of the children. Her final point is that if one judges only by language competence, one will not know the full extent of what the children can do and what they know. However, it is easy to judge the children as incompetent because it is difficult to access competency without language. In this third narrative, Sarah constructs herself as a good mother for observing her children and giving them credit for what they do know how to do—for not seeing them "as two year-olds" and coming to learn about their competencies through observation. This process, as she noted in the first narrative, began on the trip home in the Amsterdam airport and has continued as she has gotten to know about her children.

Constructing Children's Past Kinships and Histories

Perhaps a more obvious gap in knowledge for adoptive parents of older children from abroad is knowledge about their past histories, kinships, and family heritage. The question of adoptee lineage or family tree is one that is relevant for almost all adoptees and has led to more open adoptions and transparent adoption processes for adoptees in the United States and other countries as the knowledge of family history is important not only for adoptees' identities, but also for their medical history and potential problems they might face. In the following excerpt, John, who had learned Russian prior to the adoption of his two boys from Ukraine, researches his oldest son's first name on the internet using his knowledge of Russian and Cyrillic. In this conversation, John makes suggestions to his son about where his name is used and where he might be from. While the son resists a lot of this talk (a pattern that was common in this family, Fogle, 2012), the research provides an opportunity to discuss the children's histories, their ethnic and linguistic backgrounds, and create a sense of belonging that crosses the old and new family contexts. In doing this, John is able to construct multiple kinships for the children with an understanding of kinship as dynamic and situated in time and space (and language).

In Excerpt 4.4, John is searching the internet for information about his oldest son's name. The child's real name ("Dima" is a pseudonym) is unique as it is not a common Russian name, and it is also a homonym with an English word that has been impossible to replicate with a pseudonym. I have omitted parts of the following conversation and changed the names of the places they are talking about because this information would reveal the child's identity. In the examples below, I have used the pseudonym "Dima" in place of the name they are researching (i.e., Dima, Tajikistan is not a real place to my knowledge). However, the family is aware that Dima's given name is not Russian and is trying to find other examples of the name (in Cyrillic) through Google. This was in the early 2000s, and there was only limited access to such information on the internet. The excerpts from the following conversation do not represent a narrative per se, but are rather an attempt by the father to start to construct a narrative about Dima's father through the internet research.

Excerpt 4.4 Your dad

(May 2006)

1	John:	Oh, isn't this interesting <hushed, excited>?
2	Sasha:	What?
3	Dima:	What?
4	J:	Well, this is,
5	S:	D. I. M. A. [Dima]!
6	D:	[Whatever]
7	J:	This makes sense.
8		Dominic Ivingo giving Dima. Other photos. See, we thought that your dad was probably from either Tajikistan or in one

of those, and this, the very first one is, it's a, it's a place. Dima, Tajikistan.

9	D:	Should I press on it?
10	J:	Hold on.
11	S:	Tajikistan! Whoo whoo whoo.

John refers to "your dad" in Line 8, not referring to himself but rather talking about the son's birth father, and this reinterprets the category of "your dad" as either being multiple—that is, an individual can have more than one dad—or being a category to which he himself doesn't belong. By not referring to "birth dad," John further validates Dima's past kinship relationship and authenticity of both fathers. In many cases in the data I have, John often played the role of observer or listener when his children talked about their past lives, and here, like Sarah above, he is observing his child's past life—so that his role as father in the present is a role that he did not occupy in the past time.

During the conversation, John finds examples of a movie with Dima's name in it, a pet dog that had the same name and a few other items. The younger child Sasha is excited about this information and tries to copy the Cyrillic spelling of Dima's name onto his paper. Dima is less interested, but does show some engagement through the research session. At the close of the conversation, John summarizes what he found and here asks Dima what language his father spoke:

Excerpt 4.3 What language?

1	John:	That's right.
2		That's enough, Dima.
3		We just wanted to check on (.) your name.
4		So it's interesting, there are clearly some connections to Tajikistan.
5		Which we think might be where your dad is from.
6	Dima:	I don't think so.
7	J:	Where do you think he's from?
8	D:	I don't know.
9	Sasha:	Daddy, that's interesting, because,
10	J:	Na kakom yazike [on - uh - govoril on]?
11	S:	[Daddy, the first], excuse me [daddy]?

12	D:	[I don't know].
13	S:	The first,
14	J:	What language did you talk to him in?
15	S:	[Daddy, in Ukrain -]
16	D:	[I don't kno::w, daddy].
17	S:	In Ukraine, his name has four letters, but our - uh - his name in this language has,
18	D:	English, [five].
19	S:	[five].
20	J:	That's right.

Here Dima shows some resistance to his father's interest—stating that he didn't think his father was from Tajikistan despite the research (Line 2) and then repeating that he didn't know what language his father spoke. John asks about language in Line 6 for the first time in Russian, displaying his own Russian competence and perhaps trying to jog Dima's memory. Dima seems to understand the question and responds, "I don't know," in English. John then repeats the question in English, and Sasha tries to respond in English, "in Ukrainian," but doesn't get a chance to finish. Dima is annoyed because he was taken off his computer game in order to do the Google search about his name and seems to be making a complaint about that instead of engaging in the topic at hand. Sasha, who did not learn literacy skills in Russian or Ukrainian before the adoption, continues his interest in writing in Cyrillic and compares the Russian version of Dima's name to the English version, noting that there are more letters in English at which point John talks about the different alphabets with them. Here the research about the children's past and effort to connect past kinships and lives to the present also provide an opportunity for biliteracy instruction and comparison of the two languages for the younger child.

While this might not have been the most successful interaction in John's eyes, it is a good example of how multilingualism and multiple kinships coincided in this family. Without John's competence in Russian (which he learned prior to the children's adoption), researching the children's possible origins and heritage in this way would not have been possible. And while in this episode both children seem fixed on topics at hand (a computer game and the Cyrillic writing system) that are important to them, John does open the family conversation here to the possibility of having two fathers and multiple kinships in different contexts. He further connects those kinships to language and multilingual possibilities as Dima's history, kinship relations, and own linguistic background are unknown. Being a good father in many of the examples from this family's data was tied to acknowledging and constructing a new type of family that allowed multiple relationships, ways of doing, and languages in the family sphere.

Kinship as Shared History

The two data excerpts presented in this chapter centered on the construction of adopted children as possessing prior knowledge and histories that were unknown to the adoptive parents in the current context. This aspect of the unknown is a part of adoptive parenting that has typically been construed as contributing to risk or disadvantage for adoptees and their families (Brodzinsky and Schechter, 1990). Because the past is unknown, the future is hard to predict. The parents in this chapter, however, expressed contradictory opinions to this point of view in their conversations. By constructing her children as competent in her narrative about the airport and yard work, Sarah established that her children had learned valuable skills in the orphanage and could do more than she had originally thought or that she was able to deduce from their language competence. She further connects this coming-to-understanding as a part of her own acceptance of herself as a good mother. In being able to convey to me as a researcher that she has learned this important fact about her children (that the children know more than they can convey in English), she demonstrates her sensitivity toward and advocacy of her children as well as her own ability to rely on their prior knowledge.

In the second excerpt, John actively engages his two boys in researching their backgrounds through Google searches of the first son's unique name. While the oldest son rejects much of John's suppositions about his biological father's country of origin, this talk allows John to acknowledge to his sons that they have two fathers (biological and adoptive) and that they have multiple belongings and complex histories that are worthy of acknowledgment. Such processes are also relevant to transnational and transmigrant children who are not adopted but may experience multiple kinships and belongings in different times and spaces.

In both of these examples, language is a key to forming different family constructions and rejecting norms about adopted children and adoptive families. While Sarah could have accepted my discourse about multilingualism in the adoptive family, in the end, she pointed out to me that it wasn't necessarily language that mattered in forming a family but rather establishing intersubjectivity through observation and learning. For John, language was the key to researching and identifying his children's histories. His knowledge of Russian and the Cyrillic alphabet made internet research possible. His acceptance of his children's multiple kinships and complex histories also allowed for more negotiation of what it meant to be a family for himself and his children. Multilingual families are made up of monolingual, bilingual, and multilingual family members (Li Wei and Zhu Hua, 2016). Examining when family members talk about language in family conversations and interviews can serve to connect other family processes (such as constructing family membership and competencies) to the mono-, bi-, and multilingual processes that are also in play.

Narrative analysis of family conversations has helped to understand how family members construct moral stances, police behavior, and create family identities (Ochs and Capps, 2001). Here a different kind of family process is occurring that is closely tied to the kinships and multilingualisms these two families experienced. For the monolingual mother who could not easily communicate with her children, the narrative she tells about learning how to learn about their competencies is a space to construct her own position as a good adoptive mother over the time and space of the embedded stories. For the bilingual father whose competence in Russian provided a resource to research his children's prior histories and kinships, the potential or possible narrative that he would like to construct about Dima's father becomes a way to acknowledge and validate the children's pre-adoptive past and family. In short, language is tied to kinships through the narrative activities of these families, and through reconstructing past events both parents demonstrate how bi- and multilingualism as well as language learning shaped kinship processes in their families.

5

Gender, Sexuality, and Bilingualism in the LGBTQ+-Identified Family

To my knowledge at the current time, there is no published study of multilingual family language in the LGBTQ+-identified family. Scholars have investigated queer bi- and multilingual identities (Cashman, 2017; Wright, 2017), queer migration and queer citizenships (Murray, 2014; Luibheid and Cantu, 2005), globalization and queer language (Leap and Boellstorf, 2003), as well as sexual identity in TESOL (Nelson, 2009; Paiz, 2019) that point to the importance of queering bi- and multilingual studies and language teaching and learning as marginalized queer voices can point to the role of gender and sexuality in contexts of language contact. Language practices in the nuclear family can socialize children into certain gendered patterns (Merrill et al., 2014; Ochs and Taylor, 1992), and LGBTQ+-identified parents (or parents with LGBTQ+-identified children) do a lot of discursive work to normativize same-sex or transgender kinships in relation to perceived norms (Eng, 2010).

Queer investigations of language socialization have further noted the importance of gender in particular in family routines (Wagner, 2010). Furthermore, Rowlett (2020) argues that queering second language socialization research can further dislodge dominant notions of "identity" and "community" through investigation of the margins. It is this disruption of a predominant focus on ethnolinguistic identities that queering the bi- and multilingual family can afford explanations of family language. In this chapter, through the analysis of published works (documentary, comedy performance, and memoirs) as well as some survey data, I show how bilingualism provides a resource for negotiating gender roles and relationships in the family and establishing kinships and belonging outside of the family of origin. This chapter examines the intersections of bi- and multilingualism with gender roles and kinship processes in LGBTQ+ families.

While I am choosing in this book to refer to LGBTQ+ families (along with single parent and adoptive) as "non-normative" because, in part, of the field in which I work, others have argued that a queer or homonormativity has emerged in recent decades. In a volume on post-structuralist approaches to kinship, Eng (2010: 3) argued that "while gays and lesbians were once decidedly excluded from the normative structures of family and kinship, today they are re-inhabiting them in growing numbers and in increasingly public and visible ways." Cashman (2017) further found that homonormativity was an important aspect of some Latinx community members' identities in Phoenix, Arizona. Given this growing normativity (within the current context of fluctuating legal battles where the rights Eng noted have been afforded are also being taken away), it seems time for sociolinguists and family discourse scholars to catch up with other work in the humanities and social sciences in studying same-sex and transgender families. Studying LGBTQ+ families in relation to multilingual family language use can foreground the role that gender and sexuality play and further inform work on both straight and queer families by pointing to power dynamics and role negotiations that intersect with language use.

It is hard to know if LGBTQ+ families have been left out of family language studies because of the recruiting methods and inclusion criteria of the research design or if the apparent lack of such families is due rather to a "don't-ask-don't-tell" kind of approach in which parents' sexuality is not considered an important factor in the study. There is a tendency in the field of applied linguistics in general to sidestep questions of sexuality as well as research with sexual minorities because of the perception that LGBTQ+-identified learners and teachers represent a minority within the minority, and their specific concerns are not relevant to larger questions of ethnolinguistic identity or language learning. While there is a growing body of work focusing on queer-identified language teachers, classroom teaching, and learners (Liddicoat, 2009; Nelson, 2009, 2010; Paiz, 2019), there is still very little work in the multilingual queer family. A handful of studies have shown how foregrounding sexuality and gender in the study of multilingualism and multilingual families in particular can reveal implicit processes that influence the negotiation of languages in the home, socialization into family external communities that influence linguistic identities, and the intersections of bilingual child rearing with gender roles in the family (and heterosexual power structures) (Cashman, 2017; Luykx, 2003; Okita, 2002). These studies have pointed to the ways in which gender can influence the learning of certain languages at home (Luykx, 2003), how bilingual parenting is a part of gendered identities and roles in the family (i.e., as women's work) (Okita, 2002), and how sexual identity can intersect with belonging in bilingual communities and learning heritage languages (Cashman, 2017).

The number of same-sex families in the United States is not small. According to a recent report issued by the Family Equality Council (2019), there are about 2 million same-sex families in the United States. Same-sex couples with children in the United States are more likely to be poorer than heterosexual couples with children, they are more likely to be couples of color than heterosexual couples with children, they are more likely to be binational (i.e., one parent is not a US citizen), and they are more likely to live in the southern parts of the United States. These results suggest that many children with same-sex parents are also growing up in linguistically, racially, and ethnically diverse families where sexuality, gender, language, and race potentially intersect, and they may be living in rural regions of the United States where support for such diversities is not as available as in more affluent urban areas. However, linguistics research has done little to understand the language ecologies of these families or the multilingual identities available to children in such environments. This study examines these issues from multiple dimensions using an author's or performer's voice as evidence for different perspectives and stances on bilingualism in the queer family.

Researching LGBTQ+ Families

Recruiting multilingual, LGBTQ+-identified parents or family members for research is difficult. LGBTQ+ centers across the United States are inundated with requests for research participants (Julia Landis, personal communication), and the members of multilingual communities might prefer to maintain their privacy in the current world climate. In addition, a level of trust and perhaps personal interaction are needed to conduct this kind of research. While I maintain friendships and contacts with people who are queer-identified parents in different bi- and multilingual communities, I have not wanted to jeopardize those personal relationships by involving my friends in my research. I have launched two separate, anonymous surveys of multilingual, LGBTQ+ parents in the hopes of meeting some families who would be willing to continue participation in a more in-depth study, but have had very little response. In a US survey that was publicized by a number of LGBTQ+ centers across the country (in New York, Texas, North Carolina, Arizona, and Tennessee, among other states), only five people responded to the survey and none agreed to a follow-up video interview. The advertisements were published by the LGBTQ+ centers and on my personal Facebook and Instagram profiles in English and Spanish and survey participation was completely anonymous. Participants could request to have the survey translated to other languages. Research within multilingual, queer communities requires trust and a certain degree of in-group membership as Cashman (2017) was able to achieve in her study of the Latinx community in Phoenix. As I have not been able to enter such a community in the region where I currently live or a place that would be feasible to research, I am turning to publicly available work for this investigation. I begin with the small amount of survey data I was able to collect in order to frame the public works and demonstrate connections between individuals' everyday lives and the experiences of the artists, performers, and writers below.

The survey responses contextualize a closer and more in-depth analysis of published works (memoir, documentary, and comedy) that take as a central theme the author's or performer's queer identity, family, and multilingual language use. In specific, I discuss American comedian Wanda Sykes's Netflix film *Wanda Sykes: Not Normal*, a Vice documentary *Raised without Gender* featuring photographer and gender activist Del LaGrace Volcano's gender-neutral family in Sweden, journalist Minal Hajratwala's chronicle of her family's migration *Leaving India: My Family's Journey from Five Villages to Five Continents*, and Cuban-Colombian American author Daisy Hernández's coming of age memoir *A Cup of Water under My Bed*. While these texts do not represent naturally occurring family language data or research data as typical of applied and sociolinguistics, they do offer a way to examine predominate themes related to being multilingual and queer in relation to kinship processes from the point of view of an author or performer who has centered their own artistic production and life choices on these topics.

Survey Responses

The few survey responses I did receive from parents across the United States pointed to areas that deserve further attention in the study of multilingual families. The three respondents who left short descriptions of their families in the survey all noted that there were intersections between language and gender in their families. This mother, who was raising their child in Spanish and English, described how they had adapted gendered endings of the kinship term "mama" to match the gendered identities of the two mothers, that is, butch (masculine) vs. femme (feminine):

Excerpt 5.1 Mama and Mamo
Respondent 1: We go by Mama and Mamo (a being the feminine and o being the masculine ending for nouns in Spanish) to reflect that one of us is femme and one butch but both Moms.

In this example a new, translingual kinship term is created to differentiate between the same-sex couple. Spanish, with its gendered inflection, affords the couple a way to linguistically construction their "mama" identities along gender lines in a way in which English, which does not have gender marking on the nouns, cannot. As in the case of Del LaGrace Volcano discussed below, here bilingualism affords new gender identities in the family.

Another respondent talked about gender identity and bilingualism in his family specifically. While this participant noted that he and his partner did not have children, I am including his response because I think it has implications for families with children. Another group of potential family language participants that have been left out of research are families who identify as family but do not have children.

Excerpt 5.2 American masculinity
Respondent 2: Multilingualism is a delicate balancing act within the United States, regardless of sexuality/gender identity, in my experience. I am European from Belgium (Fr/Du bilingual), lived in Italy for many many years, then married my American husband. Perhaps because American masculinity is so tied to NOT being bilingual, it has led to some friction, particularly as I am the one who accommodates to English and not usually the reverse. Also, his efforts to learn another language are stymied by a lack of language awareness and educational background in this country.

In this very thoughtful response, the participant notes that since masculinity is tied to monolingualism in the United States, it has been very difficult for him to negotiate a bi- or multilingual family language policy with his husband. This phenomenon is not uncommon in mixed marriages in the United States and other English-speaking contexts where mothers are the keepers of a minority language and fathers are monolingual English speakers. Okita (2002) wrote about the ways in which minority language maintenance became women's work in the family, but few studies have attributed this power dynamic to the construction and maintenance of a certain type of masculinity as the above respondent does. Such perspectives could shed light on different family language processes associated with gender socialization as well as power dynamics within the family.

One mother also pointed to the use of Spanish as an important aspect of the children's Latinx identity:

Excerpt 5.3 "It was essential"
Respondent 3: It was essential that we raise our Latinx children bilingual. I speak Spanish but am not fluent. We created a sliding-scale Spanish immersion day care at our office when our oldest was born. 6 years later all the kids who join before age 2 and stay to at least 4 are bilingual. Both Moms read to our kids in Spanish, we are part of a large multilingual, multicultural community, and we supplement this work with trips to language schools in Mexico.

This mother indicates that she does not consider herself a fluent speaker of Spanish, but because of her children's ethnic identity as Latinx, she and her partner found it "essential" to raise their children bilingual. Unlike the mixed marriage discussed above in Excerpt 5.2, this mother (who constructs herself as not Spanish dominant) portrays herself as supportive of her family's bilingualism and has put a lot of effort into making bilingualism possible for her children (i.e., by creating a new school).

This small amount of data indicates the importance of gender and sexuality in understanding family multilingual processes that the construction of femininities and masculinities and the kinship relations that go along with these identities are important to understanding why some parents learn or use another's language or why some children choose family internal vs. family external languages. These processes come to the foreground in same-sex and transgender or non-binary-parented families as these parents are potentially more aware of their gender and sexual identities and the role gender and sexuality play in all aspects of their lives.

Memoirs, Documentaries, and Performance in Multilingual Family Research

In the absence of empirical data, memoirs and documentaries are one way of looking at queer multilingual parenting that can reveal the tensions of belonging that are part of queer-identified multilingual families and possible topics for further exploration. Following Lippi-Green (2011), I have noted in a prior study of fictional accounts of queer language learning that fiction (and other types of authored work) is an important site of the construction of language ideologies (Wright, 2017). In that study, I found that metalinguistic talk about language and language ideologies in the novel can serve to "construct social relations [between characters], prompt turns of plot, and explain events that occur in the narrative" (p. 187).

In the analysis below, I examine how authors and public figures talk about or portray their own stances toward multilingualism and queer identities. In the first part of the chapter, I examine how two bilingual, queer-identified parents who are also public figures (actress and comedian Wanda Sykes and photographer Del LaGrace Volcano) construct themselves and their children as members of bilingual, queer-identified families. This analysis focuses on material from Sykes's recent stand-up routine that aired on Netflix and a short documentary about Del LaGrace and their children published by Vice. The second section of the chapter focuses on the viewpoints of adult children raised in bilingual families who came out as queer and renegotiated their relationships with their heritage languages and cultures in relation to their sexual identities. In this section, I rely heavily on Minal Hajratwala's carefully researched memoir and history of her family's migration as well as Daisy Hernández's (2014) book *A Cup of Water*. Taken together, these cultural productions represent multilingual same-sex, transgender, and bisexual parents and children who have, in public venues, found different ways to talk about their sexuality and multilingual family lives. This chapter provides further avenues for empirical research and confirms conclusions that the individual experiences of family members are more important that homogenizing discussions about multilingual families and that including queer sexualities and discussions of sexuality more directly in research on multilingual families will uncover the complex processes at play.

The Parents' View

The texts and performances chosen for analysis in this chapter represent both queer parents' and queer children's views on multilingualism in the family and the role of language in the expression of their sexualities and genders. I start with the construction of family interactions and parenting decisions related to bilingualism, sexuality, and gender from the adult perspective. First, I analyze Wanda Sykes's narrative about her role as the African American mother in contrast to her French-speaking European wife. I then turn to a different parent perspective in Del LaGrace Volcano's discussion about choosing to raise their children in a gender-neutral environment. These two texts present slightly different views of bi- and multilingualism as resources for exclusion and humor (in the case of Sykes) or inclusion and belonging (in the case of the Volcano family).

Wanda Sykes: "My Little French Family"

Comedian Wanda Sykes and her French wife Alex Niedbalski are raising bilingual French-English twins (born in 2009) together. Sykes's recent stand-up comedy has included jokes about her wife and children using French and the ways in which their French use creates (humorous) divisions in their family. On a recent interview with Sykes by Terry Gross on the US National Public Radio show *Fresh Air* (August 1, 2019), Sykes noted that her children see her as the "English" mom and her wife Alex as the "French" mom, designating linguistic rather than national or racial identities as central to her children's perception of their two mothers. This distinction points to the role of language and bilingual competencies in the same-sex parented relationship to distinguish the mothers and potentially the importance in language differences in all families as children potentially see their parents as the "majority" or "minority" speaker in ways that might be obscured by gender differences in heterosexual families.

While Sykes clearly supported her wife's use of French at home (as she notes in interviews that her children are highly proficient in French), French becomes a central theme in some of her more recent jokes that draw on the processes of inclusion and exclusion that are a hallmark of kinship building, as discussed in Chapter 1. In her stand-up comedy Netflix film, Sykes provides two anecdotes in which her children's and wife's bilingualism becomes a resource for negotiating the family actions. Sykes has presented some examples that construct her as a foreigner in her home as Black people, she notes, are "different," but "equal."

Around minute 48 in Netflix special *Wanda Sykes: Not Normal*, following a long routine about Donald Trump and jokes about the differences between White and Black people (drawing on differences in her own family), Sykes moves into a skit about Vicks Vaporub, a home remedy that has become the source of ethnic internet memes and jokes. Sykes introduces the topic of Vicks by making fun of her own grandmother's and mother's use of the remedy to cure anything (even a fictional case of Tuberculosis). In setting up the storyline this way, she draws on intergenerational knowledge, passed down matrilineally, about how to use Vicks to cure coughs.

She then moves to her own contemporary family where she uses "them" to talk about the White French speakers (her wife and two daughters) and "us" to talk about African American culture (following the jokes about her mother and sister). She begins a narrative about how she decided to use Vicks one time when her daughter had a cough and refers to "my own little French family" to provide an abstract to the narrative (you should've seen how they reacted to Vicks). The diminutive "little French" and possessive "my" signify endearment and belonging toward the family at the same time that she then distinguishes herself as an outsider and aggressor for putting Vicks (a highly potent substance with specific odor) on her daughter. The metaphor of the Black parent as dangerous develops as the narrative continues, and the daughter claims that Wanda (who she calls "mommy-boo") is burning her. As Sykes is trying to explain that the Vicks will help her breathe, she voices her daughter switching to French to call her (other, French-speaking) mother to come help. Here the participant-related code-switching (Auer, 1985) is used by Sykes not only to construct the ethnolinguistic identities of her daughter and wife, but also to continue the "us/me" vs. "them" conflict that she set up in the abstract to the narrative.

At this point, Sykes shifts into her wife's voice and uses French to tell the daughter Olivia to close her eyes (against the fumes). In doing this, Sykes demonstrates her own competence in French at the same time that she is playing with the differences and conflicts of being an African American mother in a family that is predominately White European. Playing on stereotypes of White fragility and the inability of White people to withstand pain or discomfort, Sykes makes a joke of the potentially racialized or ethnic conflicts in her own family that are a part of her daily life. She later notes that the French speakers, "y'all," eat cheese that is stronger than Vicks, drawing on an icon of French culture to dismantle the claims of fragility and aggression. In doing this she implies, "I know you are strong enough to take something that stinks, but only when it is related to your own culture and privilege."

In the performance more generally, Sykes draws on default or dominant understandings of kinship to construct herself as an outsider in her own family. Her children do not look like her, and they do not share the same language competencies. Sykes constructs herself as the outsider for humorous effect, demonstrating how her bonds and relationships in her family are outside of the norm and require the negotiation of cultural and linguistic practices. These jokes simultaneously show that she is in fact an insider through her understanding and use of French and the protest from the other family members toward her actions (and is able to laugh about it and capitalize on it).

Sykes's jokes draw on the fact that differential language competencies can create divides in relationships in family life, that one or more family members may feel a sense of exclusion or lack belonging because of language competence. While plenty of recent family language policy studies have focused on children's resistance of a parent's language choice and children's agency in switching languages in the family (Fogle, 2012), few studies contextualize these processes in relation to family relationships and more specifically parent-child relationships. In examining Sykes's self-deprecating humor and reflection on her role as a mother in these jokes, the child's switching to French takes on other meanings—that the children's competence in French is related to their French-speaking mother as protector against the strange habits of their English-speaking mother. The use of French in this narrative draws divisions and constructs Sykes as an outsider in her own family. Such perspective is most likely only one way of looking at the situation as Sykes supports her children's bilingualism, but it is a humorous portrayal of the challenges of multilingual family life that might point to phenomena often missed by researchers because of needs to protect family privacy and intimate moments. Parental narrative and the public, artistic presentation of this kind of subjective experience afford an in-depth view of the nuances of bilingual parenting through the lens of the parent's experiences and positionalities. The jokes also provide rich insight into the ways two different kinds of mothers (one aggressive and dangerous and the other intimate and caring) can be constructed in relation to racial and linguistic difference.

Del LaGrace Volcano: Raising "Hen"

A 2017 documentary published by Vice explores the family life of intersex, non-binary, gender variant, and/or transgender artist and activist Del LaGrace Volcano, who is known for their provocative photographs depicting varied genders and sexualities. Del and their partner, who is Swedish, moved to Sweden to raise their two children. In the documentary, the interviewer (a young cisgender woman) follows Del and the kids around the town in Sweden on their daily routine and spends some time filming interviews with the teachers and children at Del's child Mika's school and with Del's mother-in-law. Del's partner does not appear in the documentary.

Del states that they chose to raise their children in Sweden because of the Swedish efforts to promote gender-neutral settings for children. The documentary reviews Swedish laws that require preschools to not enforce gender stereotypes, and teachers show the interviewer on the film how they are inclusive of all families and genders in their teaching materials and classrooms. Teachers report that they do not make suggestions to children about gender appropriate toys and clothing, and they use depictions of same-sex, non-binary, and genderqueer characters in teaching. One set of worksheets in the school included superheroes taking care of babies or ballet dancing for example.

The Swedish pronoun "hen" occupies a central place in the documentary as the interviewer talks to Del's child Mika and their friends at school about Mika's gender identity. "Hen," a third gender personal pronoun, was added to the official dictionary of the Swedish language by the Swedish Academy to refer to non-binary individuals in 2015 ("Sweden adds gender neutral pronoun to the dictionary," 2015). Each day Del or the interviewer or both ask Mika what pronoun they would like to use that day. Mika says that they do not like this question, but in most cases they choose "hen." At times, Mika explains that they are not a boy or a girl to the interviewer, and in English Del uses "they" to refer to Mika in English (as I have also chosen to do). When the interviewer asks the children directly on the playground if Mika is a boy or a girl, they say "hen"—not a boy or a girl. In contrast, the child's Swedish grandmother uses "he" to refer to Mika, and suggests that Del had not given the child a choice in being non-binary. Mika's other non-binary friend (with whom they are shown painting fingernails) is referred to as "he" in Swedish and English by their parents. In addition to using third gender pronouns "hen" and singular "they" in English, Del chose the name "mapa" or a combination of ma and pa to refer to their own parental identity (similar to the Spanish-speaking parent in my survey who chose to use "mamo" above). Language in these examples provides an important resource for the construction of non-binary genders.

Language and gender, along with other cultural norms, are tied to Del and their partner's decision to move to Sweden to raise their children. At the end of the documentary, the interviewer asks Del if they are forcing their children to be non-binary (as the grandmother seemed to indicate in her interview), and Del responds that they are raising their kids just like themselves, and that is what every other family does. This claim to cultural reproduction and the intergenerational transmission of a gender-neutral lifestyle strikes at the heart of the study of kinship and language. Parental desires for their children, imaginations of what can be, and efforts to change their children's lives are all wrapped up in the language and educational choices they make when they have the economic, psychological, and legal support to do so. Del and their partner are gender and sexual minorities and have made lives as activists and queer artists. They are both White and privileged in the sense that they have been able to move to one of the most socially progressive places in the world and raise their children as they choose. Most parents do not have this luxury; however, it is important to note that Del's work as an artist and activist grew out of intense marginalization and discrimination of intersex and transgender individuals in the United States.

Both Del and their child are shown speaking Swedish and English in the documentary. The question of if they wanted to raise their children bilingually or if they would raise their children bilingually never comes up in the documentary. Del never discusses their own decisions to learn or use Swedish, and bilingualism seems to be taken as a matter of fact in the European context. Unlike Sykes above, Del does not use the stronger Swedish competence of the other family members to metaphorically divide the family, but rather uses Swedish (and its gender-neutral pronoun) as a unifier of family identity. Just as being gender neutral in physical presentation is a part of family membership, so is being bilingual. Thus, family inclusion and the process of building kinship in this gender-neutral family are related to negotiating gender norms and adopting gender-neutral (linguistic) practices.

For all of these parents, the French English biracial moms, transgender Swedish English parents, and the respondents to the survey, language is a powerful vehicle of gender and sexuality (as well as race and ethnicity). Wanda Sykes plays with the exclusionary power of her family's use of her non-dominant language at home and constructs herself as the "Black outsider" to create humor in the narrative. Kinship is a tenuous phenomenon in Sykes's routine, and the audience is never sure if she belongs in her own family because of the racial and linguistic differences (mostly marked by the use of French or French accents) that she capitalizes on. In contrast and perhaps in a more European fashion, the documentary about Del LaGrace

Volcano never talks about their or the children's competence in Swedish, and Del never mentions it in the interview segments. The family bilingualism is taken for granted, and Del is shown speaking Swedish in a few contexts—at the hair salon with the Syrian stylist for example (who is interviewed about his gender attitudes). The fact that the Swedish language affords the non-binarism that the family desires seems to entail competence in Swedish. In this way, Swedish is constructed as a vehicle for inclusion rather than exclusion for this family, not around ethnolinguistic Swedish English national or cultural identities, but around gender identities for all family members. That is, Swedish is a tool for marking non-binary genders, and therefore it is a language used by all family members. These families are unique in some ways; they are not like most families in terms of their privilege, fame, and status, but that does not mean that gender, sexuality, and multilingualism are not as closely tied in other families. It just means that researchers have not fully investigated these questions, and that high-profile queer families provide insight into what matters in family language processes.

The Children's View

Language learning memoirs have offered perspectives that applied linguists interested in second-language acquisition have drawn on for decades in an effort to explore the inner processes of language learning and different dimensions of understanding those phenomena. Rodriguez's (1983) *Hunger of Memory* for example and Eva Hoffman's (1990) *Lost in Translation* are often cited in research articles (e.g., Pavlenko, 2007) and textbooks of second-language acquisition as evidence of attentional and affective processes associated with language learning (Ortega, 2009) and have expanded to a robust study of learner narratives in language learning. As discussed above, memoirs and other published works that address topics of sexuality and bilingualism or language learning in particular are important for understanding these intersections that have not previously been researched in depth or are difficult to access and provide insight into potential avenues for empirical study. In this section, I examine the memoirs of two young bisexual writers, Minal Hajratwala and Daisy Hernández, who at times turn their narratives to the intersections of multilingualism, family, and sexuality.

Minal Hajratwala: Migrations

In her memoir *Leaving India*, Minal Hajratwala travels all over the world to interview distant family members who emigrated from India at different times to different host nations. Through these interviews, she examines her family history in relation to colonization and globalism and her own ethnic and cultural heritage. At the same time, she tells her own story of growing up in the United States in predominately White neighborhoods as an Indian child who did not fit in. The narrative itself does not center on language or multilingualism though the topic comes up in several chapters, as Hajratwala examines the role of English in the colonial setting as well as her own language learning.

Hajratwala identifies as bisexual, and in the end of the book she centers the discussion on her own coming out story and how her sexuality affected her relationship with her family. She talks about erasing her sexual identity when she returned to her parents' house from college and the fears of rejection that she held:

> A wall still stood between what I thought of as my real life and what I shared with my parents on visits home or on the phone. To avoid constant conflict, I felt a pressure to blend in again: to reassimilate with their community's values, to disappear my sexuality, to continue to look and act like the good Indian child of the Hinduism workbook, even if it was a façade. (Hajratwala, 2009: 334)

Queer-identified individuals often talk about forming "chosen" families in place of families of origin in response to rejection or marginalization. In the following excerpt, Hajratwala (2009: 334) talks about how these fears and the need to formulate responses were a motivating force in bringing queer South Asians together in the university environment:

> Every queer South Asian conference featured an emotional session called Coming Out to Parents, or Relating to Our Families of Birth, or even *Dear Mummy & Papa*. But the main purpose of our gatherings was often affirmation: to tell ourselves, against all assertions to the contrary, that we could be both Indian and lesbian, both Pakistani and gay, both Bangladeshi and bisexual; that we were neither traitors nor deviants nor heretics but merely humans trying to love. Among these peers, some of whom became close friends, I felt that perhaps I had found my own people—my home.

In this passage, finding groups where intersections of ethnic identity and sexuality were accepted and normativized is constructed as a way to create kinship "my own people" and home outside of the biological family of origin. Discussions of "family external" processes that influence "family internal" language policy and socialization rarely include discussions of external kinships that young people, especially those who identify as queer, form. Such decisions can have very real consequences for bilingual youth as rejection by parents can also mean disassociation with or loss of a heritage language (cf. Cashman, 2017).

For Hajratwala, however, finding queer Indian communities was a road to reconciliation with her ethnicity and heritage language. In the following passage, she describes how the migrations and mobility across continents that she sought to understand through writing the memoir were related to the migration of her own sexual identities. She notes that she is more able to and interested in speaking Gujarati after becoming involved in queer activist groups in her parents' home region:

> I no longer wish to be Ann, or Marie, or even Gita. After half a lifetime of subtly Americanizing the pronunciation of my name, in the past year I have begun to say it in the Gujarati way: Minal, mee-nalr. The vowels have a specific, rolling intonation; the final letter is a consonant that does not exist in English, somewhere in the borderland between "l" and "r". Each time I say my name this way, I have the sensation of integrating language itself. I have come to understand that queerness is a migration as momentous as any other, a journey from one world to the next. (Hajratwala, 2009: 321)

Family for Hajratwala is not an assemblage of caretakers and gatekeepers who are biologically related to her, but rather "[the] lovers and friends, the created family that all free queer people know, the one we construct far from our original homes" (338). It is this future life and future family that holds more possibility for Hajratwala in terms of multilingualism than her family of origin.

A second memoir of a bisexual Latina woman, Daisy Hernández, touches on issues of bilingualism and English language learning at moments in the story of Daisy's coming out and understanding and negotiating her desires. In the following passage, Daisy describes her entry into a US school and the pull-out ESL instruction that she received in her first years. The teacher had flashcards with English words on them that she used to teach:

> I look at the white woman's cards and listen to her bold English words—dog, cat, house—and there is all the evidence of what is to come in my life. I am not to go the way of the two people I long for in the thick terror of the night. The first man I love and the first woman I adore, my father and my mother with their Spanish words, are not in these cards. The road before me is English and the next part too awful to ask aloud or even silently: What is so wrong with my parents that I am not to mimic their hands, their needs, not even their words? (Hernández, 2014: 5)

Here Hernández portrays the trauma and violence she experienced as a child having to learn English in a subtractive schooling environment. Her love for her father and adoration for her mother hint at the attraction to both genders that she experiences. Unlike Hajratwala, Hernández places the responsibility of her own self-loathing and rejection of her parents' ways of talking and doing on the White English teacher and the system that required her to reject her parents. Maintaining Spanish for Hernández here is not a choice, and that decision was not made by her or her parents.

Queering Multilingual Family Studies

The importance of queering multilingual family studies is apparent in these examples as bringing the experiences of transgender and same-sex parents as well as LGBTQ+-identified children to the foreground of family language work can shed light on how linguistic identities intersect with sexualities and genders to construct inclusion, exclusion, and power relations in the family. Understanding relationships between desire, identity, and activism can further reveal how young people see themselves in relations to their parents, their extended families, and their heritage languages. Building a strong heritage language identity, for all children, also means negotiating norms about gender and sexuality and in some cases finding new belongings. In the explorations of sexuality by bisexual authors Hajratwala and Hernández, connections formed in family external communities of belonging with family internal language processes. Forming queer kinships outside of the family, especially for Hajratwala, was critical to seeing herself as Indian and Gujarati.

These kinship processes (both external and internal) are not limited to queer communities. Straight-identified and cisgender youths also negotiate gender and sexual identities along with ethnolinguistic identities, and these negotiations are related to multilingual development and use in the family (e.g., Luykx, 2003). The construction of masculinity in particular (as noted by the respondent above) is a rich site to explore how multilingualism is connected to power and dominance in the family; but more generally, more in-depth discussions of the intersections of ethnolinguistic and gender and sexual identities can lead to fruitful discussions of family internal and family external processes as well as the role of new kinships in family multilingualism.

6

The Monolingual, Nuclear Family: Erasing Melania Trump

One of the most pervasive assumptions made in the study of childhood bi- and multilingualism is that home languages are most likely lost when children start school in a community-dominant language. And while schooling undoubtedly plays the central role in children's linguistic lives and is a site of intense monolingual academic language socialization, it is not the only factor affecting a child's access to community bi- and multilingualism or multilingual identities outside of the home. Widely circulating ideologies of bilingualism and who can be bilingual that circulate in the public sphere affect children's own self-perception and can lead to children's bilingual erasure or the need to pass as monolingual (Wright, 2018). Just as other pervasive and mythological norms are constructed about families in the public sphere, monolingualism in the family is also constructed in advertising, entertainment, and the news media as the norm and, in many cases, only condition for family life. The complex family external processes that shape language ideologies and practices have not traditionally been explored in family language research, but it is these larger popular discourses that potentially create expectations for who can speak what in families and the discursive norms by which multilingual families in monolingual contexts in particular measure themselves.

This chapter examines these discursive processes in the news media in two ways. First, I analyze the use of kinship terms in a set of newspaper articles about Melania Trump's parents' citizenship ceremony to show that reference to the nuclear family avoids constructing the Trumps as an immigrant family. I then turn to the issue of Melania and Donald's son

Barron's bilingual competence and the fact that representing the family as a nuclear family also portrays the family as a monolingual English-speaking family. Taken together, these articles demonstrate how family norms are constructed in the news media.

On August 9, 2018 (amid Donald Trump's vociferous arguments against the family reunification visa program [or chain migration] and the horrific family separations that occurred at the US-Mexican border in the summer of 2018 [Shear et al., 2018]), Viktor and Amalija Knavs, parents of Melania Trump, grandparents of Barron Trump and parents-in-law to Donald Trump, were sworn in as US citizens in New York in a private ceremony with no family members in attendance. While the ceremony was not widely publicized, it received much criticism in the press because of the clear hypocrisy in Donald Trump's rhetoric and his in-laws' use of the family reunification visa program to become US citizens (Virella, 2018). Melania Trump is the first foreign-born first lady in the United States since Louisa Adams, who was born in London in 1775 (Adams et al., 2014). Melania holds the distinction of being the only first lady of the United States to speak a language other than English as a first language, and her son Barron is subsequently the first child of a president to be bilingual through bilingual parenting practices (and not schooling). While Melania's accented English and multilingual language practices have been a source of ridicule in the media, the daily realities of her bilingualism and her son's language use are rarely, if ever, noted. Most Americans don't consider the current first family in 2019 to be a bilingual, immigrant family despite the fact that Melania's trajectory, capitalization of hyperfemininity, and potential marriage migration are similar to many East European women's migration to the United States (Wiedlack, 2019). In this chapter, I examine the discursive processes involved in portraying the first family as a monolingual, nuclear family in the mainstream news media.

This chapter focuses on variation in the use of kinship terms (e.g., parents, in-laws, grandparents, daughter, etc.) in news reports and editorials covering the Knavs' citizenship ceremony. The event provided an opportunity for the media to comment on Trump's immigration rhetoric and policies and point out the hypocrisy in the fact that his relatives had gained citizenship through family reunification visas, the same policies he had recently denounced in his Twitter posts and State of the Union Address (Keneally, 2018). In the analysis below, I demonstrate how reference to certain kinship relations (e.g., "her parents" vs. "his in-laws") connects with the articles' critique of Donald Trump's immigration policies and the hypocrisy of the Knavs' obtaining citizenship through the family reunification process that Trump had vehemently denounced. By excluding the kinship of Donald Trump to the Knavs through the choice of kinship terms, the news media erase the extended family connections, immigration status of family members, and potential multilingualism of the first family. Such practices build a monolingual, nuclear family norm in the public discourse.

Covert Bilingualism and Passing

Multilingualism has been one of the last types of family diversity to be portrayed in public media in the United States. While single mothers, divorced and blended families, and LGBTQ+-identified families have been featured in television shows since the 1970s, it is only in the past few years that bilingual families have made the mainstream (Gunderson, 2018). And while there are few studies that address the issue, bilingual families are rarely mentioned in the news or in other forms of public discourse (other than in advice articles for bilingual parents). The dominance of a monolingual family norm in the United States (that is arguably perpetuated by entertainment and news media) as well as negative attitudes toward languages other than English in many cases creates a family external context in which it is not safe, acceptable, or even possible for bilingual children to identify as bilingual and acknowledge their linguistic competencies. In my own work in the Southern United States, I found that young people of color in particular reported passing as monolingual or not being accepted as bilingual because of discrimination and erasure (Wright Fogle, 2013b; Wright, 2018). In this chapter, I look to the news media to show how the dominant societal norms of monolingualism in the United States are constructed in relation to the nuclear family and, in particular, the multilingual first family currently in the White House.

Methodological Approach

In the Introduction to the volume, I discussed the fact that studies of family interaction are a necessary and integral part of understanding family language studies; however, the construction of family in public discourse is an area that undoubtedly influences family members' language ideologies and practices despite being largely omitted from analytical approaches. In an effort to consider what larger discourses about families circulate in the public sphere that might influence and affect multilingual, non-normative families, this chapter presents a qualitative discourse analysis of kinship terms in the news articles covering Melania Trump's citizenship. In particular, I examine the use of kinship terms in the articles. The more varied kinship terms used in the articles, the more critical the stance of the author toward Donald Trump. In this way, I demonstrate that reference to a nuclear family norm becomes a neutral reporting condition in this context.

Kinship Terms

Contemporary discourse analytic approaches to kinship terminology, or reference to family roles and relationships (Sclafani, 2015), take a functional or pragmatic approach in which the use of a kinship label ("parent," "father," etc.) functions in the discourse to perform certain identities or construct realities. Sclafani (2015) demonstrated how reference to family and roles was used as a framing device in political debates for politicians to construct their political identities as well as authority in certain aspects of policy making (e.g., national security). Sclafani's study demonstrated how the use of kinship terms in public discourse (political speeches) functioned to construct identities that have implications for real world phenomena—who wins an election, for example, or how history is constructed through personal narrative.

In the following analysis, I look closely at kinship terms such as "her parents" and "his in-laws" in a set of newspaper articles covering the Knavs' citizenship ceremony. I argue that articles that take a neutral reporting tone tend to refer to the Knavs as "Melania's parents," while those that are opinion pieces tend to refer to the Knavs as "Donald Trump's in-laws" and use more varied kinship terms. The use of kinship terms in this way constructs agency in the family reunification process for the Knavs (with Melania responsible in the first instance, and Donald responsible in the second) and points to the ways in which kinship terms can be used to establish a point of view and stance in the articles as well as the important connection between kinship and immigration. I then turn to discussions of multilingualism in the Trump family to show how constructing the Trump family as a nuclear family (without extended family reference) also constructs the family as monolingual.

The Data

This chapter presents a qualitative discourse analysis of the press coverage of the granting of US citizenship to Viktor and Amalija Knavs (Melania Trump's parents) on August 9, 2018. The Lexis Nexis newspaper database as well as the general Google search engine was used to locate articles with the keywords "Melania Trump," "chain migration," and "Knavs." In addition, several newspaper archives were searched individually in order to ensure a balance of liberal and conservative newspapers (see Table 6.1 below).

Table 6.1 Sources and Headlines

Source	Headline	Date	Byline	Genre
Atlanta Journal and Constitution	Melania Trump's parents become U.S. citizens, taking their oaths in a private ceremony	8/9	Shelby Lin Erdman	News
Associated Press	Meet the newest U.S. citizens: Melania Trump parents	8/9	Michael Sisak	News
Baltimore Sun	Congrats to the Knavs	8/15		Opinion
Baltimore Sun	Congratulations, Viktor and Amalija	8/13	*Baltimore Sun* Editorial Board	Opinion
Chicago Tribune	Meet the newest U.S. citizens: Melania Trump's parents	8/9	Michael Sisak (AP)	News
Chicago Tribune	Column: Melania Trump's parents are "NOT ACCEPTABLE!" President Trump said so	8/9	Rex Hippie	Opinion
New York Post	Mel's ma & pa citizens	8/10	Bob Fredericks	News

Source	Headline	Date	Byline	Genre
New York Times	Melania Trump's parents become U.S. Citizens, using "chain migration" Trump hates	8/9	Annie Correal and Emily Cochrane	News
New York Times	Melania Trump's parents ignite debate over "chain migration"	8/16	Kelly Virella	Other
Town & Country	Melania Trump's parents just became United States Citizens	8/9	Megan Friedman	Society
Washington Post	President Trump's in-laws benefited from chain migration. That's a good thing.	n.d.	Walter Kamphoefner	Opinion
Washington Post	Melania Trump's parents become naturalized U.S. citizens despite the president's hostility toward "chain migration"	8/9	David Nakamura	News
Washington Times	Melania Trump's parents are sworn in as U.S. citizens	8/9	AP	News

It was harder to find "conservative" coverage of the topic—Fox News for example did not yield any articles on its website; however, several more conservative newspapers did run stories about the event (*Washington Times* and *New York Post* above). A database of approximately fifteen articles was created in Nvivo, and the texts were coded for keywords that denoted kinship terms or family relationships and roles (Table 6.2).

In addition, a few other terms such as "chain migration" and "family reunification" were coded as well as statements that were read as ironic or satire in order to identify overlaps in the use of certain family terms with other aspects of the article's political stance.

The Nvivo software package for qualitative research was used to code and analyze the discourse data. In addition, the word frequency function was used to query individual articles and identify additional referring terms that might

Table 6.2 List of All Kinship Terms/Family References Coded

Ancestor
Children
Daughter(s)
Family
First family
Grandparents
Husband
Immediate family members
Immigrant families
In-law
Melania's family
Ma and pa
Migrant children
Mom and dad
Mr./Mrs. Knavs
Mrs. Trump
Parents
Relatives
Siblings
Son
Son-in-law
Spouse
The couple
The Knavs's/Knavses
The Trumps
Whole family
Wife

have been missed in the coding (e.g., "First Lady" and "President" were not coded in the first round because they were not references to family). Queries of individual articles were also used to identify all of the keywords or nodes coded for each text and identify patterns across texts.

"Her Parents" vs. "His In-Laws" in Reports of the Knavs' Citizenship

The articles considered for this study all used kinship terms or references to family roles and relationships (father, mother, daughter, in-law, etc.) in reporting about Knavs' citizenship ceremony, although not all articles used all of the possible terms listed in Table 6.2. A clear pattern in reference to nuclear (i.e., parents and immediate children) ("Melania's parents") vs. extended ("Donald Trump's in-laws") family relationships was found to be related to two main aspects of the articles: the genre (news vs. opinion) and the amount of commentary or subjective discussion about immigration. Articles that maintained a neutral, reporting tone tended to refer only to "Melania's parents," while those that offered commentary or critique of Donald Trump's rhetoric and policies tended to include more varied reference to extended family relationships, most often through use of the term "in-law(s)." Opinion pieces or editorials used the most varied references to family roles. I start here with an analysis of the original Associated Press (AP) article about the event that is predominately neutral and then examine two similar news reports about the citizenship story that ran in *The Washington Post* and *New York Times*. Finally, I discuss two editorials that expressed opinions about the Knavs' citizenship ceremony. In this analysis, I show the importance of the use of kinship terms and specifically those referring to extended family relationships (in-law, grandparent, etc.) to position Donald Trump as a member of an immigrant family.

"Her Parents"

The first paragraph of the AP article (Sisak, August 9, 2018) introduces the Knavs as "Melania Trump's parents" and provides a first mention of Donald Trump as "their son-in-law":

> NEW YORK (AP)—First lady Melania Trump's parents were sworn in as U.S. citizens on Thursday, completing a legal path to citizenship that their son-in-law has suggested eliminating.

These references function in several ways. First, "Melania Trump's parents" makes Melania the focal referent for the paragraph and perhaps the whole article (as this is the first paragraph that frames the further discussion) and places Melania in a possessive relationship to her parents that indexes her possible role as the sponsor of her parents' visas to the United States. In the second clause of the opening sentence, "completing a legal path to citizenship that their son-in-law has suggested eliminating," the discourse context changes (i.e., from the individual case of the Knavs to the broader discourse about immigration policy), and the focal referent also shifts from Melania Trump to Donald Trump ("their son-in-law"). The use of possessives here minimizes Donald's agency by placing Melania and the Knavs as possessors and agents of action here. Implicitly, Melania is responsible for the Knavs' visa and the Knavs have some ownership over Donald (who is their son-in-law).

At the end of the AP article (which was used as a template article for many newspapers that covered the story), Sisak noted that Donald Trump has advocated an end to the family reunification program:

> The plan ... would limit immigrants like his wife to sponsoring only their spouses and underage children to join them in the U.S.—Not their parents, adult children or siblings.

Here Sisak refers to Melania as both an "immigrant" and "his [Donald's] wife," making Donald Trump's membership in an immigrant family and ownership of the relationships clear. This pattern and shift from "Melania Trump's nuclear family" to "Donald Trump's extended family" become clearer in other articles about the event.

Variation in the Liberal Press: *Washington Post* and *New York Times*

The news reports published on August 9 in two of the largest liberal newspapers in the United States, *The Washington Post* and the *New York Times*, varied in their coverage of the event (both departing from the AP article). While both papers discussed Donald Trump's immigration rhetoric and policy, referring to "chain migration," the authors of each report focused on different aspects of the story. The *Washington Post* provided extended discussion of the ins and outs of Donald Trump's policies while the *New York Times* humanized the story with more background about Melania Trump's childhood and her relationship to her parents and family. Both articles noted the hypocrisy between the event itself and Trump's rhetoric, but the *New York Times* article focused on Melania Trump as an immigrant and the first family as an immigrant family (centering on Melania's role as a daughter in a post-Soviet context) in more nuanced and complex terms. In fact, this article was followed by an article later in the week that covered only the comments to the original report—showing the reactions of readers (most of them from immigrant families) to the Knavs' citizenship (Virella, 2018).

The *New York Times* actively constructs the Trump family as an immigrant family, of which Donald Trump is a central member. The construction of Donald Trump as husband to Melania and son-in-law to her parents humanizes the family and makes them more relatable to other immigrant families in the United States. This construction of the Trump family as an immigrant family is done through the use of kinship terms as discussed below in relation to the narratives employed by the authors to tell about Melania and her parents' past.

The *Washington Post* article did not use the term "in-law" to refer to either Donald Trump (i.e., son-in-law) or Viktor and Amalija (i.e., Donald Trump's in-laws) in its August 9 report. The first paragraph of and first mention of the Knavs in the *Washington Post* article refers only to "First Lady Melania Trump's parents" and "President Donald Trump," and the Knavs were consistently positioned as relatives of Melania, not Donald, in this article:

> First lady Melania Trump's parents became U.S. citizens in a naturalization ceremony in New York on Thursday, completing a years-long immigration process even as President Trump has called for new laws to bar Americans from sponsoring parents and other relatives.

Rather than referring to Donald Trump and his kinship relation to the Knavs, the *Washington Post* article places Melania as the focal referent and refers to Viktor and Amalija Knavs as "her family" or "her parents." As with the AP article, the omission of the extended family reference, that is in-laws, constitutes a neutral reporting style that focuses on the nuclear family relationship between Melania, the sponsor of her parents' visa, and the parents who gained citizenship. By limiting the kinship terms to "her parents," the *Washington Post* article avoids implicating Donald Trump in the sponsorship of the Knavs' visa or the citizenship process, although the *Washington Post* article is critical of Donald Trump's rhetoric and notes the hypocrisy but does not use all of the discursive strategies available (i.e., kinship terms) to implicate Donald Trump in Melania's visa process.

In contrast, the *New York Times* article uses the term "in-laws" four times to refer to Viktor and Amalija, and the first of these is found in the first paragraph of the article:

> On Thursday, his Slovenian in-laws, Viktor and Amalija Knavs, became United States citizens in a private ceremony in Manhattan by taking advantage of that same family-based immigration program.

The use of the modifier "his" and adjective "presidential" in the *New York Times* article positions the president as the focal referent from the start of this article and further places him in an agentive relationship to the Slovenian couple who attained citizenship as "his Slovenian in-laws."

Humanizing Melania Trump's Family

The *New York Times* article foregrounds the president's relationship to the Knavs and further humanizes the couple and their daughter Melania through discussion of their background and the route to citizenship that they took as they followed Melania's career. The family is constructed in a pastoral, Soviet context in Slovenia with Mrs. Knavs helping on the family farm and working in a factory and sewing her two daughters' clothes (a foreshadowing of Melania's fashion career).

> There, Mr. Knavs was a traveling car salesman and belonged to the Communist Party. Mrs. Knavs had harvested onions on her family's farm, then worked in a textile factory, and sewed her two daughters' clothes.

This is one of the few uses of the referring term "daughter" in the database of articles, and it works to personalize the relationship between Melania Trump and her parents. The associations with the word "daughter," including a sense of family obligation, are expanded in this section of the article. In addition, the post-Soviet history of the family, the younger generation's new possibilities, and the value of hyperfeminity and mobility in the form of emigration from the post-Soviet context are indexed in reference to "Mrs. Trump's" modeling career, which led to the "whole family" sensing opportunity:

> When Mrs. Trump began her modeling career, while still a teenager, the whole family sensed opportunity, according to those who knew them in Slovenia.

This is the second reference to "whole family," in the *New York Times* article. The first time it is used, it occurs in a direct quote from Donald Trump where he argues that bringing the "whole family" to the United States through chain migration is a problem and leads to increased crime. In the *New York Times* context, reference to "whole family" functions in a number of ways, first to indicate that the teenage Mrs. Trump's international success would be a boon not only to her individually, but also for her "whole family" collectively, ostensibly including her parents and sister (who lives in New York, but whose immigration status is not public or covered in the press) and second to potentially voice Donald Trump's own rhetoric from the point of view of the immigrating family.

The notion of immigration of a child as a family decision and collective opportunity was not uncommon in the post-Soviet era of the 1990s and early 2000s as many children's decisions to work and live abroad were also tied to East European parents' desires and beliefs (Pilkington, 1996; Temkina and Zdravomyslova, 2003), and decisions to immigrate on the part of children were often sanctioned or encouraged by parents. In general, this paragraph constructs Melania as a daughter in a working-class family in Slovenia whose parents' care (and mother's own skills) was reciprocated through the path of emigration—a life story that many other migrants to the United States (and especially those in post-Soviet contexts) might be able to connect with as seen in the follow-up *New York Times* article "responses."

In much the same way that the "victim narrative" that Aditi and Jenks (2018) identify in media coverage of refugees serves to humanize refugees and downplay the "threat" associated with Muslim migrants, the background on Melania's childhood and her parents' lifestyle provided in the *New York Times* report makes the immigration story more relatable and draws on discourses of children's obligation and kinship roles that are not a part of the mainstream discussions on family reunification and migration (even in the liberal press as seen in *The Washington Post* article). This article offers the most humanizing construction of Melania Trump and her family prior to leaving Slovenia, constructing the family of origin as an important resource for Melania Trump as a migrant and the act of migration as a salvation from a harder life and the migrating child as a link for the whole family. In relation to the use of kinship terms in the two articles, the *New York Times*' foregrounding of the referring term "his in-laws" along with the humanizing migration narrative allows for a richer story to unfold—one in which immigration is seen as a family event that involved all of Melania's family members as well as one in which Donald Trump plays an agentive role. Opinion pieces tended to employ reference to extended family relationships in a greater degree (as in the *New York Times* report discussed above), and construct more possibilities for family and responsibility in regard to family reunification, to which I will turn in the following section.

Extended Family Reference in Opinion Pieces

Editorials were published in the following week after the Knavs' citizenship ceremony that commented on the hypocrisy of Donald Trump's policies and stated the authors' or, in some cases, publication's stance toward the awarding of citizenship to Viktor and Amalija Knavs. These articles tended to be ironic or humorous, borrowing Trump's Twitter posts or other language to construct a parody, for example, *Chicago Tribune* headline, "Melanie Trump's parents are 'NOT ACCEPTABLE!' President Trump said so," or they were informative with the intention of educating the public about immigration history and law (i.e., immigration historian Walter Kamphoefner's piece in *The Washington Post* discussed below). In this section, I will examine the constructions of family in two editorials published in *The Washington Post* and the *Baltimore Sun* to show how the use of kinship terms functioned to at once support the Knavs' citizenship and construct contradictory, ironic, and negative stances toward Donald Trump's immigration rhetoric.

Kamphoefner's History of Immigration

Kamphoefner's *Washington Post* editorial, "President Trump's in-laws benefited from chain migration. That's a good thing." published on August 13, provides a primer on immigration law that includes discussion of his own German ancestors and the history of immigration in the United States. Kamphoefner's article is primarily a history with reference to important laws and processes over the past century or more. There is little reference to the actual current event of the Knavs' citizenship, and the referring terms used to denote kinship relations and roles reflect the content of the piece (referring, for example, to "relatives," "ancestors," etc.).

In the body of Kamphoefner's article and his discussion of the history of immigration to the United States and the anti-chain migration lobby FAIR (that pre-dated Donald Trump according to Kamphoefner), Kamphoefner maintains a general reference to "family members," and "relatives," rather than specific familial relationships (such as "mother" and "daughter" as seen in the *New York Times* article above). Using this general form of reference avoids signifying a specific relationship that would validate chain migration (i.e., parents and children) and side-steps Donald Trump's insistence on the "nuclear family" as the migratory unit, for example rather than referring to "parents" and "children," Kamphoefner chooses the term "sponsoring relatives":

> So the argument promoted by groups like FAIR, contrasting migrants who come based on family connections with those who come based on their ability to contribute, is a false one. Not only does this mistakenly equal ability with education level, it ignores the fact that sponsoring relatives are likely to encourage relatives to join them because they have found a rewarding economic niche and want to share this opportunity with their family. But whether based on ignorance or prejudice, Trump's crusade against chain migration is a solution to a nonexistent problem.

However, when referring to the Knavs in this editorial, Kamphoefner almost exclusively uses the referring term "Donald Trump's in-laws." The first mention of the Knavs in the editorial introduces "President Trump," and "his in-laws Viktor and Amalija Knavs."

> President Trump has long railed against "chain migration" and continues to threaten to end family-preference immigration visas, despite the fact that his

in-laws Viktor and Amalija Knavs were granted U.S. citizenship through the first lady's sponsorship.

This choice of referring terms (whether conscious or unconscious) prioritizes the role of extended family members in chain migration as well as Donald Trump's agency in the process. He also refers to the "First Lady" as the sponsor of the visa, and this is the only mention of Melania Trump in this article, which serves in contrast to the other news reports above in which Melania was the focal reference of much of the reporting.

Kamphoefner's opinion piece is clearly a refutation of Donald Trump's discourse and policies on immigration, and Donald Trump remains the primary referent in discussion of current events. In the continuation of the article, "President Trump" is shortened to "Trump" (used in less formal/less respectful contexts), and reference to the Knavs continues as "his in-laws" or "Trump's in-laws." By omitting Melania from the potential pool of grammatical referents, Kamphoefner implicitly constructs Donald Trump's relationship with the Knavs as important to their immigration trajectory. This is central because it highlights the role that US-born citizens play in creating possibilities for immigration for extended (non-biological) family members and Donald Trump's own responsibility in representing and acknowledging the benefits of these processes to himself personally and to the nation:

> I do not begrudge Trump's in-laws their immigration and citizenship based on family preference visas. They are following the old American tradition of chain migration that also brought my ancestors here. All I ask is that they refrain from (as Thomas Nast captioned his 1870 cartoon skewering Irish and fellow German immigrants agitating for Chinese exclusion) 'throwing down the ladder by which they rose.'

Kamphoefner's editorial is a carefully crafted history of immigration that at the same time normalizes "chain migration" and prioritizes the role of the extended family, "in-law" relationship of the US citizen in providing visa support for family reunification. A second editorial published in the *Baltimore Sun* further strategically employs reference to kinship to point out hypocrisy in the event.

Varied Kinship Reference

On August 13, an article titled "Congratulations, Viktor and Amalija" was published online by the *Baltimore Sun*. A Lexis Nexis newspaper search found a similar article published in the print newspaper on August 15 titled "Congrats to the Knavs." The second article, which was almost identical aside from the headline, was used for the analysis in this study. The byline of the online article is "The *Baltimore Sun* Editorial Board," attributing the opinion to the whole staff.

This article uses perhaps the most diverse set of kinship terms of any of the articles, referring to "grandparents," "siblings," "daughter," and "in-laws" among others. In fact in the opening (third paragraph) introduction of the Knavs, the authors delineate the family relationships of all of the characters in the article, including terms "father-in-law," "mother-in-law," "grandparents," and "his son":

> The Knavs are, of course, President Trump's father-in-law and mother-in-law, grandparents of his son Barron and parents of first lady Melania. Mr. Trump didn't attend the ceremony despite being on vacation. Sadly, neither did Melania. It would be silly not to recognize the reason. The Trumps and the Knavs didn't want to bring extra attention to the moment because it so firmly and clearly contradicts the assault on "chain migration" that Mr. Trump has used to inflame public fears of immigrants.

These relationships are constructed around "President Trump" as a central referent who is in possession of these extended and immediate family members (as designated by the use of possessive case and pronouns). As in *The Washington Post* editorial discussed above, "his in-laws" is important because it centralizes President Trump (and not Melania) as the main relative of the Knavs and the central figure behind their citizenship and thereby brings the hypocrisy of Donald Trump's rhetoric in relation to this event into focus.

In addition to using a diverse set of kinship terms, the article also refers to migrants in a variety of ways: "undocumented immigrants," "outsiders," and "new arrivals," which denote the different belongings and identities migrants experience in the United States. The acknowledgment of the marginalization and discrimination migrants face through listing of labels that place immigrants as outsiders constructs a point of view sympathetic with the immigrant experience. This solidarity with the immigrant point of view is reinforced in the final lines of the article, in which the editorial board additionally uses a Slovenian word to criticize Trump:

> That he lives with such obvious evidence of the success of "chain migration" under his own roof makes him what his in-laws might call a *tepec*.

This use of Slovenian designates alignment with the immigrant point of view, and in fact the Knavs' point of view, by using the Knavs' own language and pointing out the value of multilingualism in expressing ideas or thoughts that might not be readily available in English.

In sum, the two editorials examined here discussed the benefits of family reunification programs and worked to normalize "chain migration" in the public discourse. In order to make these arguments, the authors referred to multiple and varied kinship relations that centered Donald Trump as the focal referent for the article, implying his agency in the immigration process of his parents-in-law, the Knavs. In contrast to the neutral reporting discussed above, in editorials the term "Melania Trump's parents" was not used frequently, and a much more complex picture of nuclear and extended family relationships that indexed family obligations, relationships, and bonds that influence transmigrant families developed in the opinion pieces. The construction of kinship relations in the articles about the Knavs citizenship ceremony serves to also construct Donald Trump's extended family membership, his agency in the Knavs' obtaining citizenship, and the hypocrisy of this action in relation to his anti-chain migration rhetoric. The erasure of extended family ties of the first family in the media further constructs the family as a monolingual English-speaking, nuclear family.

The Multilingual First Family

Language is rarely mentioned in the mainstream media's coverage of the Trump family despite the fact that Melania has been quoted to say that she speaks multiple languages and that her son also speaks Slovenian as well as other languages. In fact, all of Donald Trump's children have been reported to be proficient in a language other than English through either parenting or schooling (as the Bilingual Kidspot blog reported in 2016). In contrast to other world leaders, this omission is somewhat important as Canadian Prime Minister Justin Trudeau's bilingual family has been the topic of headlines and other presidential families' multilingualism is taken for granted. The topic of language does come up in the *Town and Country* article mentioned above and blogs where the author is motivated by this question. *Town and Country* mentions language in relation to Barron Trump's relationship with his grandparents:

> Barron is very close to grandparents, with whom he reportedly speaks Slovenian, and *Politico* described them as "hyperinvolved" in his life.

While there is a negative spin on this depiction of his grandparents as "hyperinvolved," the image of grandparents as caregivers and the important role grandparents can play in heritage language learning processes are acknowledged here. Barron's bilingualism is further highlighted in a *Bustle* article by an author who claims a bilingual identity herself:

> There's little surprise that Barron would speak multiple languages: his mother is a Slovenian immigrant and many immigrant parents (mine included) teach their children their native tongues. He's also currently being educated at [an incredibly expensive prep school] ... in Manhattan, and language skills are often critical in that type of education. In fact, Barron and Melania reportedly intend [to stay in Trump Tower] ... until at least the end of Barron's school year so he can remain at his Upper West Side prep school and keep disruption of his life to a minimum.

Here Melania is referred to as "mother" and "Slovenian immigrant" and then grouped into a category of "immigrant parents" (to which the author's own parents belong). These categories are related to language ideologies (i.e., immigrant parents teach their children their native tongues) and further attached to the elite (multilingual) schooling Barron was receiving in New York.

In these two examples, the subject of Barron's language competence is tied to his family relationships—his closeness to his grandparents in the *Town and Country* article and his mother's own language ideologies in the *Bustle* article. These articles construct the first family from the point of view of the son Barron whose mother is an immigrant and grandparents are Slovenian-speaking caregivers. This depiction is familiar to other immigrant families where extended family relationships are important to children's bilingualism, and multilingualism is important to schooling, but the first family as "immigrant" family or "multilingual" family is not a categorization that is readily available in the public discourse. Talking about Barron's grandparents entails talking about their immigration history and their multilingual caregiving. However, multilingualism is largely left out of discussion of the Trump family because of political and ideological discourses in the United States.

The Consequences of Erasing Multilingual Families

In the Introduction to this book, I noted that popular television shows in the United States had made a big shift in their depiction of diverse kinships and multilingual families. The presumably non-fiction, objective news media, however, seem to have not kept up in this change. Could fiction be a better representation of the reality of twenty-first-century families? In this chapter, I have shown how the Trump family is constructed as a monolingual, nuclear family in neutral reporting in US newspapers. I have demonstrated that a more varied use of kinship terms in newspaper articles connected with more critical stances toward Donald Trump's immigration rhetoric and policies as well as more humanizing and relatable narratives of Melania and her parents as immigrants to the United States. The implicit discourse strategy used in some of the articles to refer to the Knavs as "her parents" rather than "his in-laws" made the erasure of extended family ties, immigration status, family multilingualism possible, and the norm in public discourse. Discussions of Barron Trump's relationship with his grandparents and language competencies in other sources entailed discussion of his "immigrant mother" and multilingual childrearing, but these identities were not available in the discussion of the citizenship ceremony even in the liberal press.

These representations provide some example of how children growing up in bilingual families (even very elite ones) may not see themselves in the public sphere and, along with the negative stereotypes assigned to immigrants, choose to pass as monolingual (cf. Wright, 2018). This point is important as we consider the experiences of multilingual youth in the United States and other contexts. In these data, close relationships with grandparents and the use of multiple languages are extraordinary and perhaps negative, and these constructions represent monolingual "discourses in place" (Scollon and Scollon, 2004) that circulate in the wider society. The first multilingual parent and family occupy the US White House; however, this reality is downplayed in the news media both implicitly and explicitly. The denial of kinship ties, immigrant identities, and multilingualism is a phenomenon that affects children in multilingual families in the United States. The current rhetoric to limit the immigrant first family to its nuclear family relationships has implications for the ways in which multilingual children see themselves and the public identities available to them.

7

Researching and Supporting All Families

The twenty-first century has ushered in an age of kinship where, as de Pina-Cabral and Luetloff-Grandits (2012: 387) put it, the study of families and households of the twentieth century has given way to a return to diverse family configurations and kinship processes because of the advent of new possibilities for family formation and kinship—through reproductive technology, adoption, and same-sex and transgender parenting. Marriage is losing popularity globally, extended families and social networks take on new significance in caregiving in the context of divorce, and adoptive and queer families challenge family norms. In his 2020 review, Furstenberg calls for a return to the field of kinship studies as a way to understand these twenty-first-century processes. Kinship has further emerged in the public sphere in the center of political debates over migration and citizenship and in contemporary representations of family in popular entertainment.

Even as I am finishing this manuscript, I go to see the final *Star Wars* (*The Rise of Skywalker*) movie where the heroine Rey is, in the final scenes, instructed by the evil Lord Palpatine to reject her chosen family, her friends in the Resistance alongside whom she fights, and embrace her biological grandfather and right to the throne. On a more serious note, definitions of kin and family are central to the restrictive and oppressive policies of the current US president who advocates for an end to the family reunification visa program and has separated more than 1,500 children from their parents at the US border according to *The Washington Post* (Sachetti, 2019). And while shifts are occurring in anthropology and sociology as noted above, research in family language continues to consider family configurations alternative to the nuclear family as somewhat dispreferred or from a deficit approach (Obied, 2010; Poveda et al., 2014). Renewing a linguistic study of kinship, and more importantly kinships in bi- and multilingual, transnational, and Indigenous settings, that employs practice-based approaches and integrates kinship processes with language use will lead to more complex understandings of childhood bi- and multilingualism as well as language maintenance and shift.

The primary aim of the diverse data, texts, and analyses presented in this volume has been to connect multilingual family language studies with critical kinship studies to demonstrate how analysis of family construction in single parent, adoptive, and LGBTQ+-identified families could further expand theoretical discussions in linguistic investigations of bi- and multilingualism. Chapter 2 took a structural approach to understanding how family configuration influenced both the interactional patterns and the role of children in family conversations and family life. I considered why single parents might feel more success in raising bilingual children in terms of both the interactional environment of the single parent family and the parent-child relationship that can occur in single parent homes. Chapter 3 expanded the discussion of single parent families by examining a daily routine that engaged the use of the minority language, Russian, between a single mother and daughter. From an outcomes-based perspective, single parents raise the interactional level of their children who serve as the primary conversational partner to the parent at home. From an experience-based perspective, the collaborative and egalitarian environment of the single parent family could also contribute to using the minority language for constructing affiliation between parent and child as seen in Chapter 3 with Elena and her daughter Maria. In sum, the data in these sections contradict common stereotypes of single parents as lacking in time or resources to maintain a heritage language and point in new directions for understanding the role of family configuration as well as gender and sexuality in children's interactional agency and parenting ideologies (not just language ideologies) related to family language processes.

Kinship processes such as building a harmonious bilingual relationship and constructing children as equal interlocutors and co-collaborators in the family contextualized the use of minority languages as well as the interactional patterns in the single parent families. Similarly, in my discussion of adoptive families (Chapter 4), I demonstrated how the construction of children's histories and competencies (necessary for relationship building and validation of the children's pre-adoptive lives) drew on the family's bilingual competencies as well as one parent's understanding of what it meant to be monolingual in a multilingual context. John was able to use his own knowledge of Russian (which he learned as a second language prior to the adoption) to research his children's genealogical past, while Sarah acknowledged she had to find new ways of knowing about her children where no shared language or history allowed her access to their past lives and experiences. The need to construct shared histories, past kinships (e.g., the biological father in John's case), and understandings of competencies are not unique to adoptive families, but they are often overlooked in family language studies where the focus is generally on the here-and-now use of the minority language. These examples provide a sense of how kinship processes on longer timescales draw on multilingual resources to revisit the past, a phenomenon that is relevant to relationships with grandparents and other extended family as well as birth parents, and what is lost when family members lose access to a first language. In these examples, how multilingualism is experienced for adoptive parents and adopted children relates to their construction of family histories and reconstruction of competencies and identities.

Multilingualism is also an important resource for the construction of gender and sexuality in LGBTQ+-identified families, and bilingual resources in particular provide a way of reproducing queer cultures in LGBTQ+ families where normative gender roles and identities are often rejected as was seen with some of the survey data and Del LaGrace Volcano's family in Chapter 5. In addition, bilingual resources constructed family inclusion and exclusion in these families where language became an in-group identity marker (the use of Swedish gender-neutral "hen" in Del LaGrace Volcano's family) as well as a marker of exclusion and difference (code-switching to French) in the case of Wanda Sykes's French-English bilingual family. Multilingual family identities can also be erased when a family steps into the public sphere in the United States as was demonstrated in Chapter 6 in the analysis of the media coverage of Melania Trump. In these public constructions of family (in documentaries, performances, and the news media), the type of family portrayed (queer, lesbian, heterosexual/nuclear, harmonious, contradictory, etc.) depended on depictions of bilingualism and monolingualism to achieve the family construction. Wanda Sykes's comedy routine would not be funny if she did not voice her daughter's use of French to complain about her actions. Donald Trump's rhetoric about immigration and his monolingual, nuclear family would not be believable if newspapers also reported that his son was bilingual in Slovenian and English and that all of his children spoke a language other than English. In short, in the public sphere at least, what kind of family you are depends on the languages that you speak.

Three Ways Families Do Family

The studies in this volume have located kinship processes and family construction at three main levels: talk about family, the use of kinship terms, and participation in everyday routines. First, instances where family members talked about being family—in John's Russian language research about his son's biological father for example or in Minal Hajratwala's discussion of creating a chosen family and connections to learning a heritage language—can provide rich sites of family construction that allow for interactions among language, relationship, and identities. Such moments provide insight into long-term processes in which the heritage or minority language provides a resource for connection with new contexts and belongings. Talk about family provides moments of kinship development, constructing belonging, and also opportunities for bi- and multilingual language use. In order to know how family members view their family (as John allowed his children to acknowledge multiple kinships) or the public discourses that families respond to, examining the discursive construction of family is an important place to start.

Related to talk about family, the studies in this volume also explored the use of kinship terms in discourse to examine how they functioned across contexts to construct rapport, manage conversations, and create political stances in public discourse. The function of kinship terms in multilingual family interaction is still a relatively unexplored area of research but one that could lead to important understandings of the construction of belonging (and potentially power or distance) as children and parents make decisions about how, what, and when to call each other. In the data presented in these chapters, the collective first-person pronoun "we" coincided with single parents' construction of a collaborative family identity with children. Calling "mom" in Chapter 3 allowed one daughter the opportunity to gain the floor and negotiate the topic of conversation, and the contrast of "her parents" and "his in-laws" in news article about the Knavs' citizenship in Chapter 6 connected with maintaining a neutral reporting position or humanizing Trump's own immigrant family. Further investigations that connect the use of kinship terms to multilingualism could focus on their relationship to language negotiations and exclusion and inclusion in the family.

A third way to investigate the construction of kinship and family is to investigate the everyday routines of the family. Interactional routines are an important area of focus for language socialization studies (Garrett, 2004; Ochs and Schieffelin, 1984) and point to the connections between cultural norms (typical interactional events) and everyday language use in families. Elena and Maria's routine walk to school in Chapter 3 was not indicative of a cultural norm in the United States (as the number of families walking to school is low); however, it was representative of the family's Russian heritage (where walking to school is a norm) and, in addition to that, provided an interactional time and space for mother-daughter bonding as well as Russian language use. As a single parent, Elena had organized the family life around routines such as this (walk to school and summer trips to Russia) where she could ensure the protection of Russian in the family environment. For this reason, perhaps, she appeared more confident and calmer about her family language policy and daughter's competence in Russian than many mothers or parents in family language policy studies. Walking to school was a routine activity that was part of the mother-daughter identity, a space for the daughter to ask questions and discuss her own developing identities, and a time to use the heritage language. Other routine activities such as carpool, mealtimes, texting at bedtime, FaceTime calls, and even playing video games can involve constructions of kinship and multilingual language use in a family's everyday life. Such activities, studied longitudinally, can provide further insight into family formation (what families do every day) and family language use.

Further recent studies that incorporate data collection methods across time and space, following non-residential parents, extended family members, and children's trajectories, can expand knowledge of how families do family and the kinship processes involved in language development and use. Coetzee's

(2018) multi-sited investigation of bilingual children in South Africa calls into question the perceived responsibility of adult caregivers in the child's language socialization. Gallo's (2017) study of Mexican American families separated by deportation demonstrates the shifts in family language policies and the language ideologies of children in the context of family change. Palviainen (2020) documents multilingual digital parenting practices and the use of technology in maintaining family relationships and languages. Furthermore, Lexander and Androutsopoulos (2019) provide new tools for visualizing and representing transnational and translingual family practices. Primary to these approaches is an effort to capture not only the language practices in the child's primary home or household, but the ways in which kinship is constructed and maintained across time and space through language.

Gender and Sexuality in Family Language Policy

The studies in this volume point to the importance of gender roles and identities in family language use and multilingualism in the family. From both outcomes- and experience-based approaches to family language policy, gender and sexuality play a role in the input, interaction, and negotiation of multilingual resources in the family. Work conducted specifically with bi- and multilingual families has investigated more nuanced, subjective intersections of gender, sexuality, and family multilingualism. Okita (2002) for example offered nuanced discussion about the challenges of bilingual parenting as "women's work" and demonstrated the added burden of language socialization on language minority mothers for whom maintaining a heritage language was equated with being a good mother. Furthermore, Lanza's (1992) study of English-Norwegian bilingual families in Norway concluded that fathers (who were dominant speakers of the majority language and worked outside of the home) were important factors in the use of English, the minority language, at home. The discussions from survey data in which a Belgian American participant links monolingualism to masculinity in Chapter 6 and the example of the Trump family where heterosexuality, masculinity, and the nuclear family construct a monolingual norm point to a need for further considerations of the construction of gender in multilingual family research. In particular, fathers, masculinity, and power are important areas that link to family multilingual use.

In early work in language policy and planning, Corson (1993) noted that the study of language policy in education is generally a question of gender. He argued that women and girls in particular faced marginalization in schools because of their gender. While Luykx's analysis is not specifically on inequity and social justice, her study of Aymara in Bolivia provided nuanced analysis of gender socialization in relation to multilingual family language socialization. Luykx (2003: 26) noted:

> Gender is a central organizing principle in every human society ... Thus the relationship between gender and language socialization in bilingual contexts should not be seen as a rarified and exotic topic.

Luykx found that the segregation of men's and women's work related to who learned what and children's play mirrored adult gender roles and language use. Gender roles and socialization are one aspect of the individual experience of family language processes that are also deeply entwined with kinship processes and relationships in the family sphere as seen most clearly in the relationship building between Elena and her daughter in Chapter 3 and the LGBTQ+-identified parents in Chapter 6. These processes are also relevant to heteronormative, cisgender, nuclear families as gender roles and power negotiations influence who speaks what in the family, how languages function to negotiate roles and power, and whose work it is to manage these processes.

Gender is further an integral part of migration, a context most often studied in the study of multilingual families. Mahieu et al. (2015: 11), for example, argued that "gender relations influence migration at all levels," and that the "complete migration experience is a 'gender' phenomenon." While gender relations in countries of origin (e.g., lack of opportunity, experiences of abuse, and repudiation as a result of divorce or widowhood, as Mahieu et al. note) can provide the motivation for women to emigrate, gender relations, roles, and identities also change as a result of migration. These power dynamics influence mothers' own language learning and identity transformations (Norton, 2013) and have implications for children's development and integration, particularly for single mothers and LGBTQ+-

identified parents. Furthermore, children experience gendered patterns of socialization that can vary across households and national contexts.

In general, the study of language policy generally omits questions of gender and sexuality in favor of discussions of ethnolinguistic identity or language ideologies despite the fact that many arenas or contexts in which language policy play out are gendered and the bi- and multilingual interactions within them relate to the construction of gendered identities (Fogle and King, 2014). The intersectionality of gender, race, ethnicity, and language policies deserves greater attention and theorization across areas of linguistics, including understanding bilingualism and bilingual classroom interactions. It stands to reason that family interactions would also benefit from this approach and that, in fact, gender and sexuality (in relation to power negotiations and belonging) are central to the family language socialization and policy.

Expanding Family Language Policy

Focusing on kinship, gender, and sexuality in the study of multilingual families calls into question definitions of family language policy and language policy more generally that are often invoked by researchers studying multilingualism in the home. Spolsky (2004) argued that there are three main aspects to language policy: language ideologies, planning, and practice. While many studies in multilingual parenting focus on only one (or maybe two) of these areas (mainly the connection between language ideologies and practices), shifting the perspective of research from ethnolinguistic to other identities and questions demands a slightly broader view. From a language socialization perspective, language use and parental interactional strategies are embedded in larger cultural norms, including beliefs about children and childrearing as well as (as demonstrated in the studies in this book) gender and sexuality. For example, the Volcano family used "hen" as a way to reproduce the gender-neutral (or gender ambivalent) lifestyle of the parents and socialize children into gender-neutral norms in Chapter 5. Russian language use played a role in constructing past kinships and histories, and parents talked about language in relation to their other belief systems—children's learning, their cognitive capabilities, and their gender and sexuality in Chapter 4. Language ideologies are not sufficient to explain the complex relationship between parents' beliefs (about their children and about language) and their language practices and management. Linguistic anthropological approaches of language socialization and nexus analysis that can capture different dimensions of family life and public discourse to demonstrate the connections between societal norms, family values, and linguistic practices offer promising approaches. Furthermore, the inclusion of public discourse, artistic work, and the news media can further locate multilingual families who participate in research within larger societal processes.

Implications for Researchers, Parents, and Educators

This book grew out of a perceived need for more inclusive research designs and recruitment methods in family language studies that would shift the focus from the nuclear, cisgender, heterosexual, biological family to more varied family configurations (cf. Macalister and Miravahedi, 2017). I have argued that such a shift would foreground new processes associated with kinship, gender, and sexuality in relation to multilingualism that are relevant to all families. In this volume, I have focused on single parent, adoptive, and LGBTQ+ families because these families represent a group in which the construction of kinship is particularly salient and relevant in family interaction (e.g., Poveda et al., 2014; Fogle, 2012; Wagner, 2010) and because all three groups are subjected to stereotypes and marginalization in which the authenticity of the family unit, the capabilities of parents, and even their morality are questioned. All of the families documented in the studies in this book could be considered elite or privileged in terms of racial, ethnic, education, or social status; however, all of these families also represent sexual and family minorities within multilingual minorities and call into question the biases and normative approaches in family language research.

There are a number of other diverse family configurations that are not included here—extended, blended, and transnational families are of note, who interact using digital communication—have varying competencies in one another's languages, and establish diverse belongings and desires related to migration and family (cf. King and Lanza, 2017; Lexander and

Androutsopoulos, 2019; Palviainen, 2020). These families stay connected and negotiate belongings using multilingual resources and multiple modalities.

It is important to look beyond two-parent, heterosexual, cisgender, biological families and include all families in our research design (even those perhaps without children), to offer clear justifications for family recruitment in methodology sections, and to conduct complementary research (i.e., if one study includes only dual parent families another is focused on single parent families). Family members should be asked to define their own kinships and important figures in their family life just as the activities captured for study should be determined in collaboration with the family as in Chapter 3. Such introductory discussions can help to understand the extended family networks, external kinships, and gender roles that intersect with multilingualism.

The recruitment of diverse families, such as LGBTQ+-identified families, for family language studies is not easy as I have discussed in Chapter 6. Julia Landis of the Fort Lauderdale, FL LGBTQ Center (personal communication) notes that LGBT centers are inundated with requests for research that make it hard for the centers to honor all of them. However, the importance of advertising family studies on lists and groups where all families might have access (including LGBTQ+ parenting sites) can ensure that all families have the opportunity to participate. In addition, there should be justification of the exclusion of certain families from a study and, if possible, complementary studies conducted by the researchers that would then include the families who were left out. In sum, I am arguing that all families need to be given the opportunity to participate in multilingual family studies, and researchers should make this clear in their reporting of their study. In short, if family language researchers are excluding certain types of families in their research design, whether implicitly or explicitly, they are not providing a comprehensive account of language in the family, are missing important theoretical constructs, and are limiting what counts as a legitimate family.

What Parents Need to Know

The findings from the studies and analyses have implications for parents and educators who are raising and working with bi- and multilingual children in diverse family configurations. First and foremost, the discussions in this book are aimed at normativizing diverse families and family experiences. The families in this book represent norms that have emerged or are emerging in the twenty-first century, but they are not necessarily new as structures of caregiving and family realities have changed across time (Coontz, 2016). In relation to multilingualism in the family, the chapters in this book have argued that single parent, adoptive and LGBTQ+-identified families have different experiences with language than other parents, and that the findings from and advice given to nuclear families with two cisgender, heterosexual parents do not fit non-normative families where interactional patterns, gender roles, and relationships are different.

Single parents need to know that being a busy single mother or single father who works in the evening does not preclude raising bilingual children (as in Chapters 2 and 3). Two parents are not necessary for promoting bilingualism in the home. Bilingualism can be fostered through social networks, sibling interaction, non-residential parents, and other contexts of language use as discussed in Chapters 2 and 3 of this volume. In addition, single parents who speak a minority language can find routine activities during the day when it feels comfortable and safe to use the language. Such routine events provide a space for bilingual conversation and an expected time of use where rules and negotiations are not as necessary. Single parents can also feel reassured in their exclusive use of their own first languages in the family and the positive contribution this input makes in raising bilingual children. Another aspect of single parenting that is important for single parents to be aware of is that accommodation to children, which is more common in single parent contexts (Chapters 2 and 3), can provide useful interactional environments for children to acquire another language. While such accommodations may not be necessary to promote bilingualism, it is useful to know that allowing children joint decision making and collaboration in the family can lead to positive outcomes (cf. Coontz, 2016).

Adoptive parenting is associated with discourses of risk as I discussed in my earlier work, and the adoptive parents of transnational children in the early 2000s often did not have a wealth of research on which to base their parenting decisions. A body of scholarship on belonging for adopted children and kinships in adoptive families has emerged as a result of these processes

(Eng, 2010; Higgins and Stoker, 2011; Yngvesson, 2010) that emphasizes the need for adopted children to connect with their past identities and reconstruct their own histories and belongings. The adoptive parents in Chapter 4 forged kinships and constructed themselves as good parents in examples where they learned about their children's past competencies and histories. Acknowledging and bridging children's past and present lives is an important aspect for all multilingual families, and particularly those in transnational contexts, as contexts of language use shift over time and place, and talking about being a family and diverse kinships over time and space can be a resource for use of a minority language (as discussed in Chapter 4 as well as Chapter 3).

LGBTQ+-identified multilingual families can use multiple languages to create new norms. LGBTQ and transgender parents who are bilingual have linguistic repertoires that can facilitate the construction of new genders and kinships as seen in Chapter 5. Third gender pronouns and the creative use of gender-inflected forms can help bilingual family members create and negotiate gender roles and relationships. Unfortunately, bilingual LGBTQ+ families are not as visible in the public sphere as perhaps single or adoptive parent families are, and this remains a highly understudied population. Maintaining sexual, ethnic, and linguistic minority status can be difficult as Minal Hajratwala noted in her memoir, and for sexual minority youth forging kinships outside of the family in relation to ethnic and racial identities as well as sexualities can be an important step in forming heritage language affiliation. In the multilingual LGBTQ+ families discussed in Chapter 5, bi- and multilingualism provided resources for belonging, inclusion, and exclusion and parents in multilingual LGBTQ+ families may provide a model of how to provide accepting and inclusive environments for gender-neutral language use and connecting language heritage with new identities.

Finally, parents need to be aware of the societal pressures their children will face for being bi- or multilingual (particularly in contexts such as the United States). Monolingualism is connected to nuclear family configurations, as we have begun to see in some family language research where it is that the extended family members play an important role in providing access to minority languages (e.g., Smith-Christmas, 2016; Curdt-Christiansen, 2016). More than that, examinations of public discourse about families can complexify the field of family language studies by connecting family interactions with dominant (monolingual, nuclear) norms that circulate in the public discourse as seen in Chapter 6 where family multilingualism is erased in the public sphere and children in particular feel pressure to "pass" as monolingual outside of the home (Wright, 2018).

What Teachers Need to Know

School is an important site of socialization that often, as researchers in bi- and multilingual families know, counteracts the language socialization work done at home. Teachers can take away three main points from the analyses and discussions in this volume. First, stereotypes and evaluations of single parent, adoptive, and LGBTQ+-identified families that might assume that bilingualism is too time-consuming for these parents or that bilingualism complicates the other aspects of being in a minority family should be rejected. Non-normative families benefit from bi- and multilingualism as resources for family bonding, constructing genders and sexualities, accessing the past and building the future, and constructing kinships within and without the nuclear family as well as constructing family belonging and identity especially in transnational families. Linguistic diversity and diversity in family configuration worked together for the families in this volume and presented important sites for children's development and identities.

Second, educational research points to the importance of building relationships with students in teaching and learning. More specifically, work with Latinx youth has focused on the role of an ethics of caring in schooling processes (García et al., 2013). Allowing children to reflect on the intersections of their own family and kinships with their language competencies ("Why are my languages important to me?" "With whom do I use what languages?") can further draw connections between home and school.

Third, teachers who are also single moms, multilingual, and/or queer can support their students by addressing their own identities in their teaching. While being "out" is not always possible in all environments and should be only a teacher's individual and personal choice, a teacher's own identity can serve to reduce the marginalization of children in the classroom who might feel different or not recognize their own situation in the class around them or the teaching materials (Paiz, 2019).

Implications for Activists

Finally, in the current political climate of family separations in the US, Brexit, and Russian encroachment in world events, there is still little awareness about multilingual families in the public discourse. Activists do not fill the streets arguing for more rights for multilingual families or recognition of the bilingual competence of children. The erasure of family multilingualism is potentially tied to a host of other discourses that construct toxic masculinity, heteronormativity, and the dominance of the nuclear family in the public sphere as I demonstrated in Chapter 6. Erasing multilingualism erases immigration and mobility, extended family relationships, and the role of the minority language-speaking mother and creates an "as-if" naturalized norm of the monolingual, nuclear, citizen family. Immigration is tied to gendered processes, and Melania Trump provides a primary example of the ways in which hegemonic monolingualism, heterosexism, and anti-feminism constrain her own linguistic identities. While Melania Trump is a controversial figure because of the choices she has made, she is not unlike other post-Soviet women who immigrated in the 1990s and early 2000s who, while being seen as opportunistic, were also tied to their families of origin and instrumental in providing a better life for other family members through the transnational value placed on Slavic femininities. The silencing of her own and her son's multilingualism in public (including ridicule of her accented English) is a form of oppression that remains invisible in our current public debates and considered unremarkable because of her own privilege and perceived choice in the matter. The representation of the Trump family as a monolingual family in the press and public sphere is damaging to the multilingual children growing up in the United States who are given further cause to stay invisible, pass for monolingual, and limit their family language use to the interior of their homes.

Critical Multilingual Kinship Studies

It is time that the study of family language caught up with other areas of the social sciences in centering kinship processes as a way to understand the language practices, decisions, and ideologies of family members. Kinships are formed and enacted inside and outside of households, with biological relatives and with strangers, through monolingual and multilingual language use. Kinship processes are integral to understandings of belonging, inclusion (and exclusion), and identity as well as caregiving and socialization. The feeling of kinship, the family bond, and the activities involved in doing family can shape and are shaped by how and what languages are used.

The studies in this volume focused on talk about family by family members, the discursive and interactional functions of kinship terms, the role of routines in constructing family relations, and the bi- and multilingual resources used in LGBTQ+-identified families. Implications for researchers, parents, and teachers include ways to include non-normative families in research, advice on understanding the affordances and benefits of being a non-normative parent in a multilingual context, and how to promote an understanding and validation of complex kinships and multilingualism in the classroom. Finally, the volume also examined the pervasive monolingual ideologies that erase multilingual families in contexts such as the United States and argued for more discussion of such erasures in relation to the construction of masculinity, dominance, and heterosexism in the public sphere. There is no family language if we are not including and examining all possible forms of family.

References

Adams, L., Hogan, M., and Taylor, C. J. (2014), *A Traveled First Lady: Writings of Louisa Catherine Adams*. Cambridge: Belknap Press: An Imprint of Harvard University Press.

Aditi, B., and Jenks, C. J. (2018), "Fabricating the American Dream in U.S. Media Portrayals of Syrian Refugees: A Discourse Analytical Study," *Discourse and Communication*, 12(3), 221–39.

Adler, P. A., and Adler, P. (1984), "The Carpool: A Socializing Adjunct to the Educational Experience," *Sociology of Education*, 57(4), 200–10.

Al Zidjaly, N. (2009), "Agency as an Interactive Achievement," *Language in Society*, 38(2), 177–200.

Andreassen, R. (2016), "Online Kinship," *MedieKultur: Journal of Media and Communication Research*, 32(61), 76–92.

Archambault, C. (2010), "Fixing Families of Mobile Children: Recreating Kinship and Belonging among Maasai Adoptees in Kenya," *Childhood*, 17(2), 229–42.

Auer, J. C. P. (1985), *Bilingual Conversation*. Amsterdam: John Benjamins.

Berko Gleason, J. (1975), "Father and Other Strangers: Men's Speech to Young Children," in D. Dato (ed.), *Georgetown Roundtable on Languages and Linguistics*, 289–97. Washington, DC: Georgetown University Press.

Blommaert, J., Collins, J., and Slembrouck, S. (2005), "Spaces of Multilingualism," *Language and Communication*, 25(3), 197–216.

Blum-Kulka, S. (1997), *Dinner Talk: Cultural Patterns of Sociability and Socialization in Family Discourse*. New York/London: Routledge.

Blum-Kulka, S. (2008), "Language Socialization and Family Dinnertime Discourse," in N. H. Hornberger (ed.), *Encyclopedia of Language and Education*, 2661–73. Boston: Springer.

Brodzinsky, D. M., and Schechter, M. D. (1990), *The Psychology of Adoption*. New York: Oxford University Press.

Brown, R. (1996), *Against My Better Judgement: An Intimate Memoir of an Eminent Gay Psychologist* (1st edition). Binghamton, NY: Harrington Park Press.

Caldas, S., and Caron-Caldas, S. (2002), "A Sociolinguistic Analysis of the Language Preferences of Adolescent Bilinguals: Shifting Allegiances and Developing Identities," *Applied Linguistics*, 23(4), 490–514.

Canagarajah, A. S. (2008), "Language Shift and the Family: Questions from the Sri Lankan Tamil Diaspora," *Journal of Sociolinguistics*, 12(2), 143–76.

Cashman, H. (2017), *Queer, Latinx, and Bilingual: Narrative Resources in the Negotiation of Identities*. New York/London: Routledge.

Cline, T., De Abreu, G., O'Dell, L., and Crafter, S. (2010), "Recent Research on Child Language Brokering in the United Kingdom," *MediAziono: Journal of Interdisciplinary Studies on Language and Cultures*, 10, 105-24.

Coetzee, F. (2018), "Hy leer dit nie hier nie ('He Doesn't Learn It Here'): Talking about Children's Swearing in Extended Families in Multilingual South Africa," *International Journal of Multilingualism; Abingdon*, 15(3), 291-305.

Coontz, S. (2016), *The Way We Never Were: American Families and the Nostalgia Trap* (revised, updated edition). New York: Basic Books.

Corson, D. (1993), *Language, Minority Education, and Gender: Linking Social Justice and Power*. Clevedon: Multilingual Matters.

Cruz-Ferreira, M. (2006), *Three Is a Crowd?: Acquiring Portuguese in a Trilingual Environment*. Clevedon: Multilingual Matters.

Curdt-Christiansen, X. L. (2009), "Invisible and Visible Language Planning: Ideological Factors in the Family Language Policy of Chinese Immigrant Families in Quebec," *Language Policy*, 8(4), 351-75.

Curdt-Christiansen, X. L. (2013), "Family Language Policy: Sociopolitical Reality versus Linguistic Continuity," *Language Policy*, 12(1), 1-6.

Curdt-Christiansen, X. L. (2016), "Conflicting Language Ideologies and Contradictory Language Practices in Singaporean Multilingual Families," *Journal of Multilingual and Multicultural Development*, 37(7), 694-709.

De Fina, A. (2003), *Identity in Narrative: A Study of Immigrant Discourse*. Amsterdam: John Benjamins Publishing Company.

De Houwer, A. (1999), "Environmental Factors in Early Bilingual Development: The Role of Parental Beliefs and Attitudes," in G. Extra and L. Verhoeven (eds.), *Bilingualism and Migration*, 75-96. Berlin and New York: Mouton de Gruyter.

De Houwer, A. (2007), "Parental Language Input Patterns and Children's Bilingual Use," *Applied Psycholinguistics*, 28(3), 411-24.

de Pina-Cabral, J., and Leutloff-Grandits, C. (2012), "The Importance of Kinship in Contemporary Anthropological Research," *Ethnologie Française*, 42(2), 8.

Döpke, S. (1998), "Can the Principle of 'One Person – One Language' Be Disregarded as Unrealistically Elitist?" *Australian Review of Applied Linguistics*, 21(1), 41-56.

Eng, D. L. (2010), *The Feeling of Kinship: Queer Liberalism and the Racialization of Intimacy*. Durham: Duke University Press.

Enriquez, L. (2016), "'I Talk to My Family in Mexico, but I Don't Know Them': Undocumented Young Adults Negotiate Belonging in the United States through Conversations with Mexico," in M. Friedman and S. Schultermandl (eds.), *Click and Kin: Transnational Identity and Quick Media*, 27-47. Toronto: University of Toronto Press, Scholarly Publishing Division.

Family Equality | LGBTQ Family Building Survey (2019), Family Equality Council. Available online: https://www.familyequality.org/resources/lgbtq-family-building-survey/

Fishman, J. A. (1991), *Reversing Language Shift*. Clevdon: Multilingual Matters.

Flores, A. (2018), "The Descendant Bargain: Latina Youth Remaking Kinship and Generation through Educational Sibcare in Nashville, Tennessee," *American Anthropologist*, 120(3), 474–86.

Fogle, L. W. (2012), *Second Language Socialization and Learner: Adoptive Family Talk*. Bristol/Buffalo: Multilingual Matters.

Fogle, L. W. (2013a), "Parental Ethnotheories and Family Language Policy in Transnational Adoptive Families," *Language Policy*, 12(1), 83–102.

Fogle, L. W. (2013b), "Family Language Policy from the Children's Point of View: Bilingualism in Space and Time," in M. Schwartz and A. Verschik (eds.), *Successful Family Language Policy*, 177–200. Dordrecht: Springer.

Fogle, L. W., and King, K. A. (2014), "Gender, Sexuality, and Multilingualism in the Language Classroom," in B. Spolsky, O. Inbar-Lourie, and M. Tannenbaum (eds.), *Challenges for Language Education and Policy*, 281–93. New York: Routledge.

Fogle, L. W., and King, K. A. (2017), "Bi- and Multilingual Family Language Socialization," in P. A. Duff and S. May (eds.), *Language Socialization*, 1–17. Springer International Publishing.

Fox, R. (1984), *Kinship and Marriage: An Anthropological Perspective*. Cambridge: Cambridge University Press.

Franklin, S., and McKinnon, S. (2002), *Relative Values: Reconfiguring Kinship Studies*, Durham: Duke University Press.

Friedman, M., and Schultermandl, S. (2016), *Click and Kin : Transnational Identity and Quick Media*. Toronto: University of Toronto Press.

Furstenberg, F. F. (2020), "Kinship Reconsidered: Research on a Neglected Topic," *Journal of Marriage and Family*, 82(1), 364–82.

Gafaranga, J. (2010), "Medium Request: Talking Language Shift into Being," *Language in Society*, 39(02), 241–70.

Gallo, S. (2017), *Mi Padre: Mexican Immigrant Fathers and Their Children's Education* (1st edition). New York: Teachers College Press.

Gallo, S., and Hornberger, N. H. (2019), "Immigration Policy as Family Language Policy: Mexican Immigrant Children and Families in Search of Biliteracy," *International Journal of Bilingualism*, 23(3), 757–70.

García, O., Woodley, H. H., Flores, N., and Chu, H. (2013), "Latino Emergent Bilingual Youth in High Schools: Transcaring Strategies for Academic Success," *Urban Education*, 48(6), 798–827.

Garrett, P. B. (2004), "Review of Language Socialization in Bilingual and Multilingual Societies," *Language in Society*, 33(5), 776–9.

Garrett, P. B. (2008), "Researching Language Socialization," in P. A. Duff and S. May (eds.), *Language Socialization*, 1–17. Springer International Publishing.

Gauthier, R., and Moody, J. (2014), "Anatomies of Kinship: Preliminary Network Models for Change and Diversity in the Formal Structure of American Families," in S. M. McHale, P. Amato, and A. Booth (eds.), *Emerging Methods in Family Research*, 73–93, CITY Publisher.

Gordon, C. (2004), "'Al Gore's Our Guy': Linguistically Constructing a Family Political Identity," *Discourse and Society*, 15(5), 607–31.

Gordon, C., Tannen, D., and Sacknovitz, A. (2007), "A Working Father: One Man's Talk About Parenting at Work," in D. Tannen, S. Kendall, and C. Gordon (eds.), *Family Talk: Discourse and Identity in Four American Families*, 195–232. Oxford: Oxford University Press.

Gunderson, A. (2018), "The Rise of Bilingual Families on Broadcast Television," *Paste Magazine*, September 18. Available online: https://www.pastemagazine.com/articles/2018/02/the-rise-of-bilingual-families-on-broadcast-televi.html (accessed September 25, 2019).

Gyogi, E. (2014), "Children's Agency in Language Choice: A Case Study of Two Japanese-English Bilingual Children in London," *International Journal of Bilingual Education and Bilingualism*, 18(6), 749–64.

Habermas, J. (1979), *Communication and the Evolution of Society*. Boston: Beacon Press.

Habermas, J. (1987), *Knowledge and Human Interests*. Cambridge: Polity Press.

Hajratwala, M. (2009), *Leaving India: My Family's Journey from Five Villages to Five Continents*. Boston: Houghton Mifflin Harcourt.

Hawkins, M. R. (2005), "Becoming a Student: Identity Work and Academic Literacies in Early Schooling," *TESOL Quarterly*, 39(1), 59–82.

Heath, S. B. (1982), "What No Bedtime Story Means: Narrative Skills at Home and School," *Language in Society*, 11, 49–76.

Heath, S. B. (1983), *Ways with Words: Language, Life and Work in Communities and Classrooms*. Cambridge: Cambridge University Press.

Hernández, D. (2014), *A Cup of Water under My Bed: A Memoir*. Boston: Beacon Press.

Higgins, C. (2019), "The Dynamics of Hawaiian Speakerhood in the Family," *International Journal of the Sociology of Language*, 255, 45–72.

Higgins, C., and Stoker, K. (2011), "Language Learning as a Site for Belonging: A Narrative Analysis of Korean Adoptee-Returnees," *International Journal of Bilingual Education and Bilingualism*, 14(4), 399–412.

Hoffman, E. (1990), *Lost in Translation: A Life in a New Language* (Reprint edition). New York: Penguin Books.

Homans, M. (2018), "Critical Adoption Studies: Conversation in Progress," *Adoption and Culture*, 6(1), 1–49. JSTOR.

Jacobson, H. (2008), *Culture Keeping: White Mothers, International Adoption, and the Negotiation of Family Difference*. Nashville: Vanderbilt University Press.

Jane the Virgin. (2014–19), US Netflix. Retrieved April 23, 2020, from https://www.imdb.com/title/tt3566726/?ref_=fn_al_tt_1

Jean Berko Gleason—Unfolding Language, Unfolding Life (n.d.), The On Being Project. Retrieved September 30, 2019, from https://onbeing.org/programs/jean-berko-gleason-unfolding-language-unfolding-life/

Kamphoefner, Walter D. (2018), "President Trump's In-Laws Benefited from Chain Migration. That's a Good Thing," *The Washington Post*, September 18. Available online: https://www.washingtonpost.com/outlook/2018/09/05/president-trumps-in-laws-benefited-chain-migration-thats-good-thing/?utm_term=.ce7a7a34bcac (accessed March 13, 2019).

Kendall, S. (2007), "Father as Breadwinner, Mother as Worker: Gendered Positions in Feminist and Traditional Discourses of Work and Family," in D. Tannen, S. Kendall, and C. Gordon (eds.), *Family Talk: Discourse and Identity in Four American Families*, 123–64. Oxford: Oxford University Press.

Kendrick, M., and Namazzi, E. (2016), "Family Language Practices as Emergent Policies in Child-Headed Households in Rural Uganda," in J. MacAlister and S. Mirvahedi (eds.), *Family Language Policies in a Multilingual World: Opportunities, Challenges, and Consequences*, 56–73. New York: Routledge.

Keneally, M. (2018), "8 Times Trump Slammed 'Chain Migration' before It Apparently Helped His Wife's Parents," *ABC News*, August 10. Available online: https://abcnews.go.com/U.S./times-trump-slammed-chain-migration-apparently-helped-wifes/story?id=57132429 (accessed May 21, 2019).

King, K. A. (2013), "A Tale of Three Sisters: Language Ideologies, Identities, and Negotiations in a Bilingual, Transnational Family," *International Multilingual Research Journal*, 7(1), 49–65.

King, K. A. (2016), "Language Policy, Multilingual Encounters, and Transnational Families," *Journal of Multilingual and Multicultural Development*, 37(7), 726–33.

King, K., and Fogle, L. (2006), "Bilingual Parenting as Good Parenting: Parents' Perspectives on Family Language Policy for Additive Bilingualism," *International Journal of Bilingual Education and Bilingualism*, 9(6), 695–712.

King, K. A., and Fogle, L. W. (2013), "Family Language Policy and Bilingual Parenting," *Language Teaching*, 46(2), 172–94.

King, K. A., and Fogle, L. W. (2017), "Family Language Policy," in T. L. McCarty, and S. May (eds.), *Language Policy and Political Issues in Education, Encyclopedia of Language and Education*. Springer International Publishing, DOI: 10.1007/978-3-319-02344-1_25

King, K. A., Fogle, L., and Logan-Terry, A. (2008), "Family Language Policy," *Language and Linguistics Compass*, 2(5), 907–22.

King, K., and Lanza, E. (2017), "Ideology, Agency, and Imagination in Multilingual Families: An Introduction," *International Journal of Bilingualism*, 23(3), 717–23.

Kroløkke, C., Myong, L., Adrian, S. W., and Tjørnhøj-Thomsen, T. (eds.) (2016), *Critical Kinship Studies*. London/New York: Rowman and Littlefield.

Kulick, D. (1997), *Language Shift and Cultural Reproduction: Socialization, Self and Syncretism in a Papua New Guinean Village*. Cambridge: Cambridge University Press.

Labov, W., and Waletzky, J. (1967), "Narrative Analysis," in J. Helm (ed.), *Essays on the Verbal and Visual Arts*, 12–44. Seattle: University of Washington Press.

Lansford, J. E., Ceballo, R., Abbey, A., and Stewart, A. J. (2001), "Does Family Structure Matter? A Comparison of Adoptive, Two-Parent Biological, Single-Mother, Stepfather, and Stepmother Households," *Journal of Marriage and Family*, 63(3), 840–51.

Lanza, E. (1992), "Can Bilingual Two-Year-Olds Code-Switch?" *Journal of Child Language*, 19(3), 633–58.

Lanza, E. (1997/2004), *Language Mixing in Infant Bilingualism: A Sociolinguistic Perspective*. Oxford: Oxford University Press.

Leap, W. L., and Boellstorff, T. (eds.) (2003), *Speaking in Queer Tongues: Globalization and Gay Language*. Urbana: University of Illinois Press.

Lemke, J. (2000), "Across the Scales of Time: Artifacts, Activities, and Meanings in Ecosocial Systems," *Mind, Culture, and Activity*, 7(4), 273–90.

Lévi-Strauss, C. (1965), *The Future of Kinship Studies*. Proceedings of the Royal Anthropological Institute of Great Britain and Ireland, 13–22.

Lévi-Strauss, C. (1969), *The Elementary Structures of Kinship*. Boston: Beacon Press.

Lexander, K. V., and Androutsopoulos, J. (2019), "Working with Mediagrams: A Methodology for Collaborative Research on Mediational Repertoires in Multilingual Families," *Journal of Multilingual and Multicultural Development*, 1–18. Retrieved April 23, 2020, from https://www.tandfonline.com/doi/full/10.1080/01434632.2019.1667363?scroll=top&needAccess=true.

Li Wei (2012), "Language Policy and Practice in Multilingual, Transnational Families and Beyond," *Journal of Multilingual and Multicultural Development*, 33(1), 1–2.

Li Wei (2018), "Translanguaging as a Practical Theory of Language," *Applied Linguistics*, 39(1), 9–30. https://doi.org/10.1093/applin/amx039

Liddicoat, A. J. (2009), "Sexual Identity as Linguistic Failure: Trajectories of Interaction in the Heteronormative Language Classroom," *Journal of Language, Identity, and Education*, 8(2–3), 191–202.

Lin, A. M. Y. (2015), "Researcher Positionality," in F. Hult and D. C. Johnson (eds.), *Research Methods in Language Policy and Planning*, 21–32. Malden, MA: John Wiley and Sons, Ltd.

Lippi-Green, R. (2011), *English with an Accent: Language, Ideology and Discrimination in the United States* (2nd edition). London/New York: Routledge.

Lo, A., and Kim, J. (2011),"Manufacturing Citizenship: Metapragmatic Framings of Language Competencies in Media Images of Mixed Race Men in South Korea," *Discourse and Society*, 22(4), 440–57.

Lou, J. J. (2017), "Spaces of Consumption and Senses of Place: A Geosemiotic Analysis of Three Markets in Hong Kong." *Social Semiotics*, 27(4), 513–31.

Luibheid, E., and Cantu, L. (2005), *Queer Migrations: Sexuality, U.S. Citizenship, and Border Crossings* (1st edition). Minneapolis: University of Minnesota Press.

Luykx, A. (2003), "Weaving Languages Together: Family Language Policy and Gender Socialization in Bilingual Aymara Households," in R. Bayley and S. Schecter (eds.), *Language Socialization in Bilingual And Multilingual Societies*, 25–43. Multilingual Matters Ltd.

Macalister, J., and Mirvahedi, S. H. (eds.) (2017), *Family Language Policies in a Multilingual World: Opportunities, Challenges, and Consequences* (1st edition). New York: Routledge.

MacWhinney, B. (2000), *The CHILDES Project: Tools for Analyzing Talk* (3rd edition). Mahwah, NJ: Lawrence Erlbaum Associates.

Mahieu, R., Timmerman, C., and Heyse, P. (2015), "Gender-Sensitive Migration Research: Theory, Concepts and Methods," in C. Timmerman, M. Martiniello, A. Rea, and J. Wets (eds.), *New Dynamics in Female Migration and Integration*, 9–25. New York: Routledge.

Malinowski, B. (1930), "Kinship," *Man*, 30, 19–29.

Mather, M. (2010), *Children in Single-Mother Families—Population Reference Bureau*. Retrieved March 11, 2020, from https://www.prb.org/singlemotherfamilies/

Merrill, N., Gallo, E., and Fivush, R. (2014), "Gender Differences in Family Dinnertime Conversations," *Discourse Processes*, 52(7), 533–58.

Morgan, H. L. (1871/1997), *Systems of Consanguinity and Affinity of the Human Family*. Lincoln: University of Nebraska Press.

Murray, D. A. B. (2014), "Preface to the Special Issue: Queering Borders: Language, Sexuality and Migration," *Journal of Language and Sexuality*, 3(1), 1–5.

Navarro, D., and Macalister J. (2016), "Adrift in an Anglophone World: Refugee Families' Language Policy Challenges," in J. Macalister and S. H. Mirvahedi (eds.), *Family Language Policies in a Multilingual World: Opportunities, Challenges, and Consequences* 115–32. New York: Routledge.

Nearly Half of Russians Own Cars (2012), Radio Free Europe/Radio Liberty. Retrieved January 31, 2020, from https://www.rferl.org/a/russia_cars/24578724.html

Nelson, C. D. (2009), *Sexual Identities in English Language Education: Classroom Conversations*. New York: Routledge.

Nelson, C. D. (2010), "A Gay Immigrant Student's Perspective: Unspeakable Acts in the Language Class," *TESOL Quarterly*, 44(3), 441–64.

Nordstrom, S. N., and Plascencia, O. G. (2017), "For Your Consideration (An Introduction to Walking With): Walking With," *Reconceptualizing Educational Research Methodology*, 8(1), 14–17.

Norton, B. (2013), *Identity and Language Learning: Extending the Conversation* (2nd edition). Bristol: Multilingual Matters.

O'Mara, S. (2019), *In Praise of Walking: The New Science of How We Walk and Why It's Good for Us*. London: The Bodley Head.

Obied, V. M. (2010), "Can One-Parent Families or Divorced Families Produce Two-Language Children? An Investigation into How Portuguese–English Bilingual Children Acquire Biliteracy within Diverse Family Structures," *Pedagogy, Culture and Society*, 18(2), 227–43.

Ochs, E. (1988), *Culture and Language Development: Language Acquisition and Language Socialization in a Samoan Village*. Cambridge: Cambridge University Press.

Ochs, E. (1994), "Stories That Step into the Future," in D. Biber and E. Finegan (eds.), *Sociolinguistic Perspectives on Register*, 106–35. Oxford: Oxford University Press.

Ochs, E., and Capps, L. (2001), *Living Narrative: Creating Lives in Everyday Storytelling*. Cambridge, MA: Harvard University Press.

Ochs, E., and Kremer-Sadlik, T. (2013), *Fast-Forward Family: Home, Work, and Relationships in Middle-Class America*, Berkeley: University of California Press.

Ochs, E., and Schieffelin, B. (1984), "Language Acquisition and Socialization: Three Developmental Stories and Their Implications," in R. Shweder and R. LeVine (eds.), *Culture Theory: Essays on Mind, Self, and Emotion*, 276–320. Cambridge: Cambridge University Press.

Ochs, E., and Schieffelin, B. B. (2011), "The Theory of Language Socialization," in A. Duranti, E. Ochs, and B. B. Schieffelin (eds.), *The Handbook of Language Socialization*, 1–21. West Sussex: Wiley-Blackwell. http://onlinelibrary.wiley.com/doi/10.1002/9781444342901.ch1/summary

Ochs, E., and Taylor, C. (1992), "Family Narrative as Political Activity," *Discourse and Society*, 3(3), 301–40.

Ochs, E., and Taylor, C. (1995), "The 'Father Knows Best' Dynamic in Dinnertime Narratives," in K. Hall and M. Bucholtz (eds.), *Gender Articulated: Language and the Socially Constructed Self*, 97–120. London: Routledge.

Okita, T. (2002), *Invisible Work: Bilingualism, Language Choice, and Childrearing in Intermarried Families*. Amsterdam/Philadelphia: John Benjamins.

Organisation for Economic Co-operation and Development (OECD) (2011), *The Future of Families to 2030*. Paris: OECD.

Ortega, L. (2009), *Understanding Second Language Acquisition*. London: Hodder Education.

Otsuji, E., and Pennycook, A. (2010), Metrolingualism: Fixity, Fluidity and Language in Flux. *International Journal of Multilingualism*, 7(3), 240–54. https://doi.org/10.1080/14790710903414331

Paiz, J. M. (2019), "Queering Practice: LGBTQ+ Diversity and Inclusion in English Language Teaching," *Journal of Language, Identity & Education*, 18(4), 266–75.

Palviainen, Å. (2020), Video, Calls as a Nexus of Practice in Multilingual Translocal Families. *Zeitschrift für InterkulturellenFremdsprachenunterricht*, 25(1), 85–108.

Pavlenko, A. (2007), "Autobiographic Narratives as Data in Applied Linguistics," *Applied Linguistics*, 28(2), 163–88.

Pennycook, A. (2001), *Critical Applied Linguistics: A Critical Introduction*. New York: Routledge.

Pilkington, H. (1996), *Gender, Generation and Identity: In Contemporary Russia*. London: Routledge.

Poushter, J. (2015), Car, Bike or Motorcycle? Depends on Where You Live. *FactTank: News in the Numbers*. Pew Research Center. Retrieved March 11, 2020, from https://www.pewresearch.org/fact-tank/2015/04/16/car-bike-or-motorcycledepends-on-where-you-live/

Poveda, D., Jociles, M. I., and Rivas, A. M. (2014), "Socialization into Single-Parent-by-Choice Family Life," *Journal of Sociolinguistics*, 18(3), 319–44.

Poveda, D., Jociles, M. I., Alonso, E., and Morgade, M. (2015), N°8: Strategies for Socialization into a Non-Conventional Family Project. ETNIA-E: CUADERNOS DE INVESTIGACIÓN ETNOGRÁFICA SOBRE INFANCIA, ADOLESCENCIA Y EDUCACIÓN DEL IMA/FMEE.

Powell, I., and Montgomery, M. (n.d.), *International Adoptions Have Dropped 72 Percent since 2005—Here's Why*. The Conversation. Retrieved October 5, 2019, from http://theconversation.com/international-adoptions-have-dropped-72-percent-since-2005-heres-why-91809

"President Donald Trump and His Multilingual Family" (November 9, 2016), *Bilingual Kidspot*. https://bilingualkidspot.com/2016/11/09/president-donald-trump-multilingual-family/

Raised without Gender (2017), [Video] UK: Vice Video. Available online: https://video.vice.com/en_uk/video/vice-raised-without-gender/590c860c0ebace424fb320c9 (accessed October 4, 2019).

Riggs, D., and Peel, E. (2016), *Critical Kinship Studies: An Introduction to the Field*. Palgrave Macmillan UK. Available online: https://doi.org/10.1057/978-1-137-50505-7

Rodriguez, R. (1983), *Hunger of Memory: The Education of Richard Rodriguez*. New York: The Dial Press.

Sachetti, M. (October 24, 2019), ACLU Says 1,500 More Migrant Children Were Taken from Parents by the Trump Administration. *Washington Post*. Retrieved March 12, 2020, from https://www.washingtonpost.com/immigration/aclu-says-1500-moremigrant-children-were-taken-from-parents-by-trumpadministration/2019/10/24/d014f818-f6aa-11e9-a285-882a8e386a96_story.html

Said, F., and Zhu Hua (2017), "'No, no Maama! Say 'Shaatir ya Ouledee Shaatir'!' Children's Agency in Language Use and Socialisation," *International Journal of Bilingualism*, 23(3), 771–85.

Schiffrin, D. (2002), "Mother and Friends in a Holocaust Life Story," *Language in Society*, 31(03), 309–53.

Sclafani, J. (2015), "Family as a Framing Resource for Political Identity Construction: Introduction Sequences in Presidential Primary Debates," *Language in Society*, 44(3), 369–99.

Scollon, R., and Scollon, S. B. K. (2003), *Discourses in Place: Language in the Material World*. Oxon: Routledge.

Scollon, R., and Scollon, S. B. K. (2004), *Nexus Analysis: Discourse and the Emerging Internet*. London: Routledge.

Shear, M., Goodnough, A., Haberman, D. (June 20, 2018), "Trump Retreats on Separating Families, but Thousands May Remain Apart," *The New York Times*. Retrieved April 23, 2020, from https://www.nytimes.com/2018/06/20/us/politics/trump-immigration-children-executive-order.html

Shin, S. J. (2013), "Transforming Culture and Identity: Transnational Adoptive Families and Heritage Language Learning," *Language, Culture and Curriculum*, 26(2), 161–78.

Shin, S. J. (2014), "Language Learning as Culture Keeping: Family Language Policies of Transnational Adoptive Parents," *International Multilingual Research Journal*, 8(3), 189–207. https://doi.org/10.1080/19313152.2014.911052

Singerman, D. (2007), "The Economic Imperatives of Marriage: Emerging Practices and Identities among Youth in the Middle East," *SSRN Electronic Journal*. https://doi.org/10.2139/ssrn.1087433

Smith, M. (1933), "Influence of Age, Sex, and Situation on the Frequency, Form and Function of Questions Asked by Preschool Children," *Child Development*, 4(3), 201–13.

Smith-Christmas, C. (2014), Being Socialised into Language Shift: The Impact of Extended Family Members on Family Language Policy," *Journal of Multilingual and Multicultural Development*, 35(5), 511–26, DOI: 10.1080/01434632.2014.882930

Smith-Christmas, C. (2016), *Family Language Policy: Maintaining an Endangered Language at Home*. London: Palgrave.

Spolsky, B. (2004), *Language Policy*. Cambridge: Cambridge University Press.

Spolsky, B. (2012), "Family Language Policy—the Critical Domain," *Journal of Multilingual and Multicultural Development*, 33(1), 3–11.

Stryker, R. (2010), *The Road to Evergreen: Adoption, Attachment Therapy, and the Promise of Family* (First). Ithaca, NY: Cornell University Press.

"Sweden Adds Gender-Neutral Pronoun to Dictionary" (n.d.), *The Guardian*. Available online: https://www.theguardian.com/world/2015/mar/24/sweden-adds-gender-neutral-pronoun-to-dictionary

Takahashi, K. (2012), *Language Learning, Gender and Desire: Japanese Women on the Move*. Bristol /Buffalo: Multilingual Matters.

Tannen, D. (2006), *You're Wearing That?: Understanding Mothers and Daughters in Conversation*. New York: Ballantine Books.

Tannen, D. (2007), "Power Maneuvers and Connection Maneuvers in Family Interaction," in D. Tannen, S. Kendall, and C. Gordon (eds.), *Family Talk: Discourse and Identity in Four American Families*, 27–48. Oxford: Oxford University Press.

Tannen, D., Kendall, S., and Gordon, C. (2007), *Family Talk: Discourse and Identity in Four American Families*. New York: Oxford University Press.

Temkina, A., and Zdravomyslova, E. (2003), "Gender Studies in Post-Soviet Society: Western Frames and Cultural Differences," *Studies in East European Thought*, 55(1), 51–61.

Tovares, A. V. (2010), "All in the Family: Small Stories and Narrative Construction of a Shared Family Identity That Includes Pets," *Narrative Inquiry*, 20(1), 1–19.

Tulviste, T., and Ahtonen, M. (2007), "Child-Rearing Values of Estonian and Finnish Mothers and Fathers," *Journal of Cross-Cultural Psychology*, 38(2), 137–55.

U.S. Census Bureau News (2007), *Single-Parent Households Showed Little Variation since 1994*. U.S. Census Bureau Reports. Available online: http://www.census.gov/Press-release/www/releases/archives/families_households/009842.html

Van Mensel, L. (2018), "'Quiere koffie?' The Multilingual Familylect of Transcultural Families," *International Journal of Multilingualism*, 15(3), 233–48.

Virella, K. (2018), "Melania Trump's Parents Ignite Debate over 'Chain Migration,'" *The New York Times*, August 16. Available online: https://www.nytimes.com/2018/08/16/reader-center/melania-trumps-parents-chain-migration.html (accessed March 14, 2019).

Volkman, T. A., Johnson, K., Yngvesson, B., Kendall, L., and Cartwright, L. (2005), *Cultures of Transnational Adoption*. Durham, NC: Duke University Press Books.

Wagner, S. N. (2010), "Bringing Sexuality to the Table: Language, Gender and Power in Seven Lesbian Families," *Gender and Language*, 4(1), 33–72.

Wanda Sykes Loves Stand-Up: That's Where "I Can Be Free," She Says. (n.d.), *Fresh Air*. Available online: https://www.npr.org/2019/08/01/747103750/wanda-sykes-loves-stand-up-that-s-where-i-can-be-free-she-says

Wanda Sykes: Not Normal (2019), US Netflix. https://www.imdb.com/title/tt9169592/?ref_=fn_al_tt_1

Wiedlack, K. (2019), "In/Visibly Different: Melania Trump and the Othering of Eastern European Women in US Culture," *Feminist Media Studies*, 19(8), 1063–78.

Wilkins, D. (2018), "Kinship, Belonging, and Citizenship in Indian Country." Presentation given at the Lumbee Reform Discussion, North Carolina.

Williams, K. (2020), "The Decade in Review," *Journal of Marriage and Family*, 82(1), 7–8. https://doi.org/10.1111/jomf.12655

Wright, L. (2017), "Bilingual/Bisexual: Linguistic and Sexual Fluidity in Fictional Accounts of Bilingualism and Language Learning," *Journal of Language and Sexuality*, 6(1), 177–203.

Wright, L. (2018), "Evaluating Place in Orientations of Narratives of Internal Migration," *Narrative Inquiry*, 28(1), 198–214.

Yngvesson, B. (2010), *Belonging in an Adopted World: Race, Identity, and Transnational Adoption*. Chicago: University of Chicago Press.

Zhu Hua (2015), "Interculturality: Reconceptualising Cultural Memberships and Identities through Translanguaging Practice," in F. Dervin and K. Risager (eds.), *Researching Identity and Interculturality*, 109–24. London: Routledge.

Zhu Hua, and Li Wei (2016), "Transnational Experience, Aspiration and Family Language Policy," *Journal of Multilingual and Multicultural Development*, 37(7), 655–66.

Index

adoptees 81–3, 94, 98
   and belonging 81
   identity 94
   Korean returnees 81
   older 81
   and pre-adoptive life 87, 99, 141
   Russian-speaking 3, 82
   school-age 87
   transnational 45
adoption 11–12, 14, 34, 80, 139
   and cultural reproduction/transformation 80
   and family language 81
   open 94
   queer 79
   and risk 82–83, 98
   transnational or international 79, 83–4
   transracial 79 (*see also* critical adoption studies)
adoptive families 13–17, 22, 25–6, 31, 37–8, 79, 81, 84–5, 99, 102, 139–40, 147, 149, 151
   as negotiated family 79–80
   transnational 13, 48, 50, 57
adoptive parents 24, 38, 45–7, 50, 80, 82–5, 87, 94, 98, 149–50
   learning Russian 52
agency 122, 127, 133, 135
   child 5, 7, 18, 21, 29, 34–5, 45–6, 66, 77, 80, 111, 140

belonging 1, 10, 14, 16–7, 142, 147–51, 153
   family 14
   and immigration 16, 134
   Indigenous 16
   LGBTQ+ families 102–3, 107–8, 110–11, 117, 142
   single parent families 30, 54
   transnational adoptees 79–81, 83–5, 89, 95, 98–9
Berko Gleason, Jane 23

bilingual parenting 2–3, 5, 20, 32–3, 54, 56, 75, 83–4, 103, 111, 120, 144
biliteracy 33, 56
birth parent 141
bisexual 2–3, 23, 108
   writers 114–17
Brown, Roger 25

caregiving 1, 4, 6, 9–10, 26, 30, 34–5, 55, 80, 92, 137, 139, 149, 115
   educational 14–15
chain migration 120, 123–5, 127, 130, 132–5
CHILDES 38–9
cisgender 118, 145, 147–9
citizenship 17, 21, 81
   queer 101
   Trump family 119–23, 126–9, 131–5, 137, 139, 143
code-switching 66, 110, 126 (*see also* medium request)
collaboration 29–30, 37, 54, 126, 149
comedy 101, 104, 109
covert bilingualism 121, 149 (*see also* passing)
critical adoption studies 81–2, 84
critical kinship studies 6, 10, 12, 14, 16, 140
critical multilingual family language studies 25
culture keeping 81, 85
Cyrillic 95–7, 99

discourses in place 21, 138
diverse families 9–10, 23, 25, 103
   recruitment of 148–9
divorce 24–5, 31, 32, 47, 55–7, 121, 139, 145
documentaries 21, 107, 141
dual parent families 29–32, 34, 36, 44, 55–6, 148

elite
    bilingualism 136–7
    families 147
English as a Second Language 15, 117
extended family 10, 35, 121, 123, 141, 143,
        148, 150, 152
    Trump family 126–8, 131–7

family discourse 9, 13, 19–20, 57, 80, 102
family external
    communities 103, 117
    context 121
    discourses 26
    influences 21
    languages 107
    processes 54, 116, 118–19
    socialization 36
family formation 4, 11, 26–7, 34, 85, 139,
        143
family history 94, 115
family identity 30, 57, 64, 75–6, 79, 113, 143
family internal
    language policies 21, 116
    languages 107
    processes 54, 118
    socialization 36
family language policy 2–8, 10, 14, 18–21,
        30, 32, 35–6, 46, 60, 75, 77, 80, 106,
        111, 143–4, 146–7
family language studies 5–6, 9, 22, 26, 34,
        84, 102, 122, 140–1, 147–8, 150
family membership 17, 99, 113, 135
fathers 23, 34, 96, 98, 106, 144
    non-residential 35
    primary caregivers 38
First Lady 120, 128, 133–4 (*see also*
        Trump, Melania)
French (language) 108, 141–2

gender 1, 4–5, 9, 13, 18, 25–36, 82, 101–18
gender-neutral
    environment 108, 112
    family 104, 113
    lifestyle 113
    norms 146
    pronouns 141, 112–13
gendered language 17
grandparents 10, 12, 120, 125, 134, 141
    Barron Trump's 136–7

Gross, Terry 109
Gujarati 116, 118

Hajratwala, Minal 114–18, 142,
        150
Hen (Swedish) 111–12
heritage language 4, 30–1, 52, 103, 108,
        116–17, 136, 140–4, 150
Hernández, Daisy 104, 108, 114, 116–17
heteronormativity 152
homonormativity 102
hyperfemininity 120, 130

identity 17, 53
    children's 66, 68, 75, 112
    ethnic 116
    ethnolinguistic 146
    gender 105, 112
    good father 98
    good mother 89, 94, 98, 144
    Latinx 106
    mother-daughter 143
    parents' 112
    queer 101, 104
    sexual 103, 115
    teacher 151
    transformation 145
immediate family 125–6, 134
immigrant 15–16, 119–20, 125–8, 133–8
immigration 14, 21, 123, 152
    Donald Trump 120–1, 123, 126–34, 142
India 104, 115–16, 118
interaction 4
    and family configuration 18
    and family construction 30, 147
    and family discourse 20
    and kinship 9–10, 13–14, 26, 85–6
    language of 61
    and language shift 7–8, 32
    and language socialization 19
    and narrative 86
    parent-child 4, 58
    in single parent families 34–7, 42–4,
        55–7, 76, 140
    use of kinship terms in 66, 142
    and walking 77
interactional data 20–1, 122
interactional routines 17, 57, 75, 143
interviews 45–53

kinship 1, 6, 9, 11–18, 137, 139–40, 152–3
  and adoption 79–80
  as caregiving 14–15 and routine 65–74
  external 116
  as inclusion and exclusion 109–10, 113
  multiple 94–8
  and narrative 86
  queer 118
  as shared history 98–9
  transgender 101
kinship terms 11, 17, 21, 61, 66, 119–31, 134, 142
Knavs, Amalija and/or Victor 120–3, 125–9, 131–5, 137, 143
Korea adoptive families 81
Korean adoptee returnees 81

language input 29
language maintenance 106 (*see also* language shift)
language shift 4–5, 7
language socialization 7, 14, 17, 19–20, 57, 79
  and family language policy 146–7
  and gender 144–6
  queer investigations of 101
Latinx identities 4, 15, 102, 106
LGBTQ+ children 101, 117
LGBTQ+ families 1, 17, 25–6, 101–38, 149–50
LGBTQ+ learners and teachers 102
LGBTQ+ parents 18, 25, 101, 145
literacy 35, 38, 52, 58, 87
Lumbee Tribe of North Carolina 16–17

masculinity 106, 118, 144–5, 153
  toxic 152
media discourse 21, 119–21
medium request 32 (*see also* code-switching)
memoir 107–8
minority language 26, 29–36, 44, 54, 56–7, 77, 106, 140–2, 150, 152
mobility 25, 116, 130, 152
"mom" (calling) 13, 56 (*see also* kinship terms)
monolingual 1, 21, 83, 99, 106, 138
  normativity 26, 121
  nuclear family 120–1, 123, 135
  passing as 119, 121, 137

monolingualism 106, 144, 150, 152
mother-daughter relationship 45, 56–9, 61, 74–7, 143
mothers 21, 23
  single 31–6, 55–6
multilingual families 2–8, 18, 23, 76, 102, 107–8
  diverse 9–10, 26
  erasure of 137–8, 152
  and language competencies 85, 99
  in monolingual contexts 119
  outcomes vs. experiences 8–9, 18, 25–7

narrative 43, 45–6, 66, 74, 83–95, 98–9, 107–11
  learner 114
  migration 131
  victim 130
nexus analysis 6, 21, 147
non-normative family 4–5, 9, 14, 17, 19, 86, 102, 122, 149, 151, 153
nuclear family 10–11, 26, 35–6, 80, 101, 120–3, 135, 138
  monolingual 144, 150

one-parent-one-language 33

passing 121 (*see also* covert bilingualism)
post-soviet 128, 130, 152
pronominal reference 45, 50–3
public discourse 121–2, 135, 137, 142, 147, 150–2

questions (in family interaction) 37–44
  wh-questions 43

researcher positionality 22–5
routine (*see* interactional routine)
Russian language 2–3, 19, 38, 44, 47–64
  single parent family use 71–7
  adoptive family use 82, 94–9, 142–3
Russian identity 66–8

Scollon, Ron and Suzie 21
sexual identity (*see* identity)
single mother (*see* mothers)
Slovenia 129–30
Slovenian language 135–6, 142
Spanish language 14–15, 33–5, 105–7, 117

Sweden 104, 111–12
Swedish language 112–14, 141
Sykes, Wanda 104, 107–11

teachers 74–6, 151
timescales 58, 141
transgender 101–2, 107, 108, 111, 113, 117, 139, 158
translanguaging 66 (*see also* translingual)
translingual 105, 144
transmigrant 25, 38, 135

Trump, Barron 120, 134, 136–7
Trump, Donald 109, 120–2, 124, 126–35, 137, 142, 143
Trump, Melania 13, 21, 119–53

Ukraine 37–8, 80, 87–90, 95, 97

Volcano, Del LaGrace 111–14

walking to school 55–9, 143

www.ingramcontent.com/pod-product-compliance
Lightning Source LLC
Chambersburg PA
CBHW070641300426
44111CB00013B/2209